ALL ABOUT HORSES
HOMESCHOOLING
JOURNAL

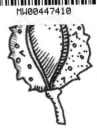

Name: & Age:

Address:

Phone & Email:

INSTRUCTIONS

What do you want to learn about horses?

1.

2.

3.

4.

5.

Action Steps:

1. Go to the library or bookstore.

2. Bring home a stack of at least SIX interesting books about horses. Choose some that have diagrams, instructions and illustrations.

Supplies Needed:

You will need pencils, black drawing pens, colored pencils, gel pens and markers.

Choose SIX Books About Horses
To Use As School Books!

1. Write down the titles on each cover below.
2. Keep your stack of books in a safe place.
3. Be ready to read a few pages from your books daily.
4. Complete 10 pages each day in this workbook.

You will need a smooth black gel pen
and colored pencils before you turn the page!

Circle Today's Date

January
February
March
April
May
June
July
August
September
October
November
December

1 2 3 4 5 6
7 8 9 10 11
12 13 14 15
16 17 18 19
20 21 22 23
24 25 26 27
28 29 30 31

MONDAY
TUESDAY
WEDNESDAY
THURSDAY
FRIDAY
SATURDAY
SUNDAY

2015
2016
2017
2018
2019
2020
2021
2022
2023
2024
2025
2026
2027
2028
2029

Write Today's Date:_____

Start Your Day!

Copy a Verse or Quote

_ _ _ _ _ _ _ _ _ _ _ _ _ _ _ _ _ _ _

_ _ _ _ _ _ _ _ _ _ _ _ _ _ _ _ _ _ _

_ _ _ _ _ _ _ _ _ _ _ _ _ _ _ _ _ _ _

_ _ _ _ _ _ _ _ _ _ _ _ _ _ _ _ _ _ _

_ _ _ _ _ _ _ _ _ _ _ _ _ _ _ _ _ _ _

To-Do List

LEARN TO DRAW HORSES

Look at the Drawing.

Trace the Drawing

Draw the Missing Parts With a Smooth Black Pen.

Draw it Yourself.

Reading Time - 1 Hour (Set a timer)

Choose TWO Books - Read from each book for 30 minutes.

Copy important words or pictures from your book here:

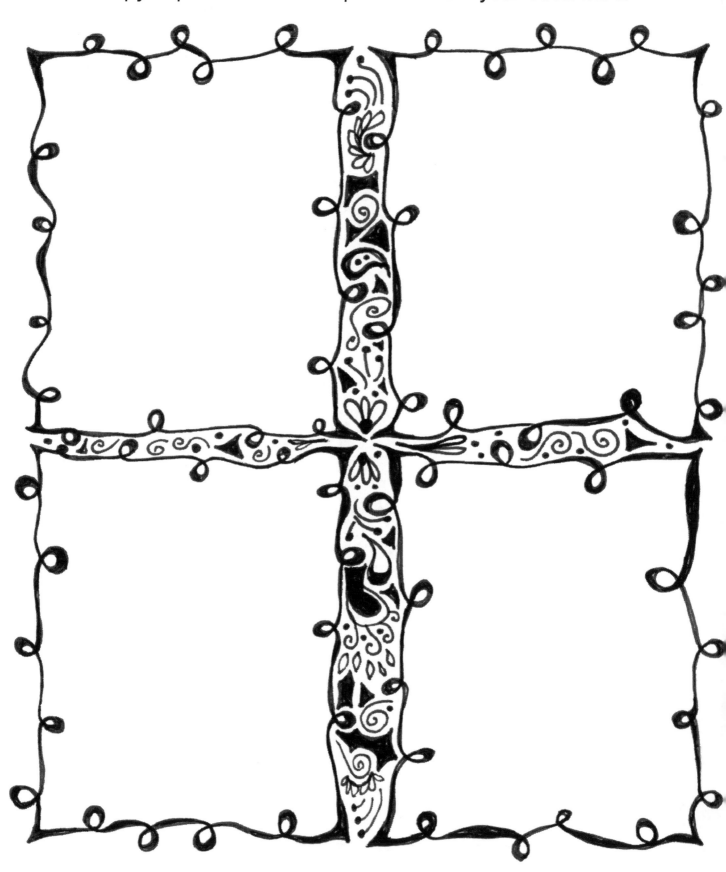

Spelling Time

Find 20 Words with **4** letters each.

Look in your books for words.

Write the words here:

Hopes, Dreams & Ideas

USE YOUR COLORED PENCILS

PRACTICE DRAWING HORSES

Circle Today's Date

January
February
March
April
May
June
July
August
September
October
November
December

1 2 3 4 5 6
7 8 9 10 11
12 13 14 15
16 17 18 19
20 21 22 23
24 25 26 27
28 29 30 31

MONDAY
TUESDAY
WEDNESDAY
THURSDAY
FRIDAY
SATURDAY
SUNDAY

2015
2016
2017
2018
2019
2020
2021
2022
2023
2024
2025
2026
2027
2028
2029

Write Today's Date: _____

Start Your Day!

Copy a Verse or Quote

To-Do List

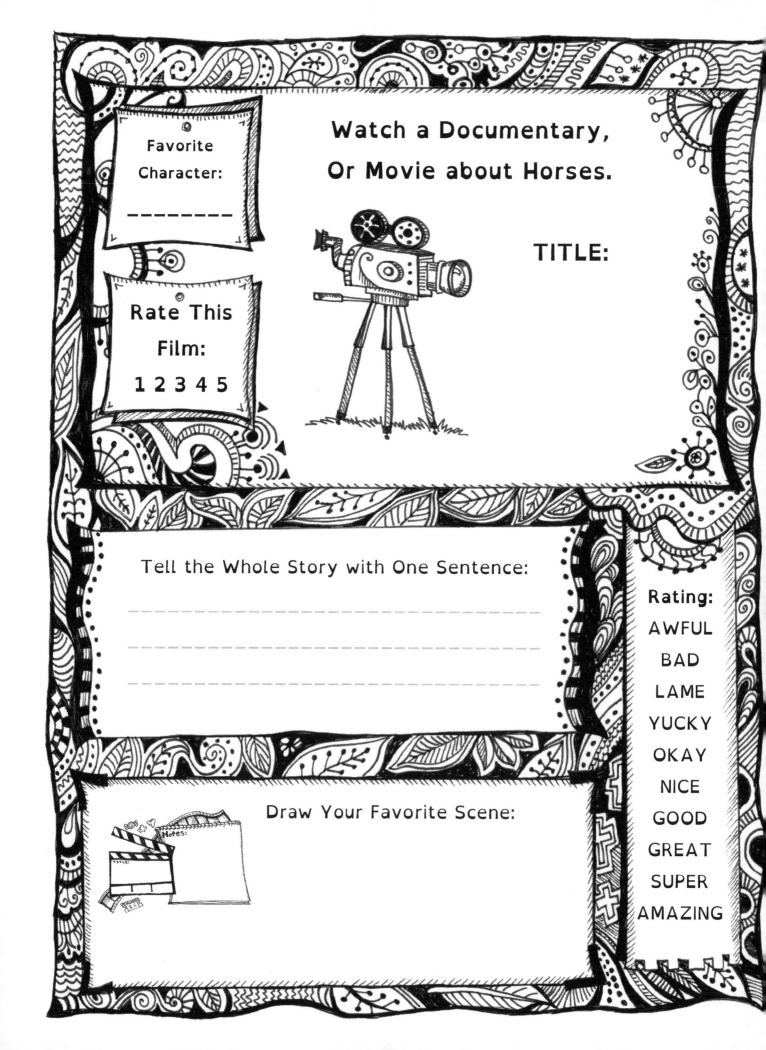

Favorite
Character:

_____

Rate This
Film:

1 2 3 4 5

Watch a Documentary,
Or Movie about Horses.

TITLE:

Tell the Whole Story with One Sentence:

Draw Your Favorite Scene:

Rating:

AWFUL

BAD

LAME

YUCKY

OKAY

NICE

GOOD

GREAT

SUPER

AMAZING

USE YOUR COLORED PENCILS

Nature Study

Go outside and make a realistic
drawing of something
you find in nature.

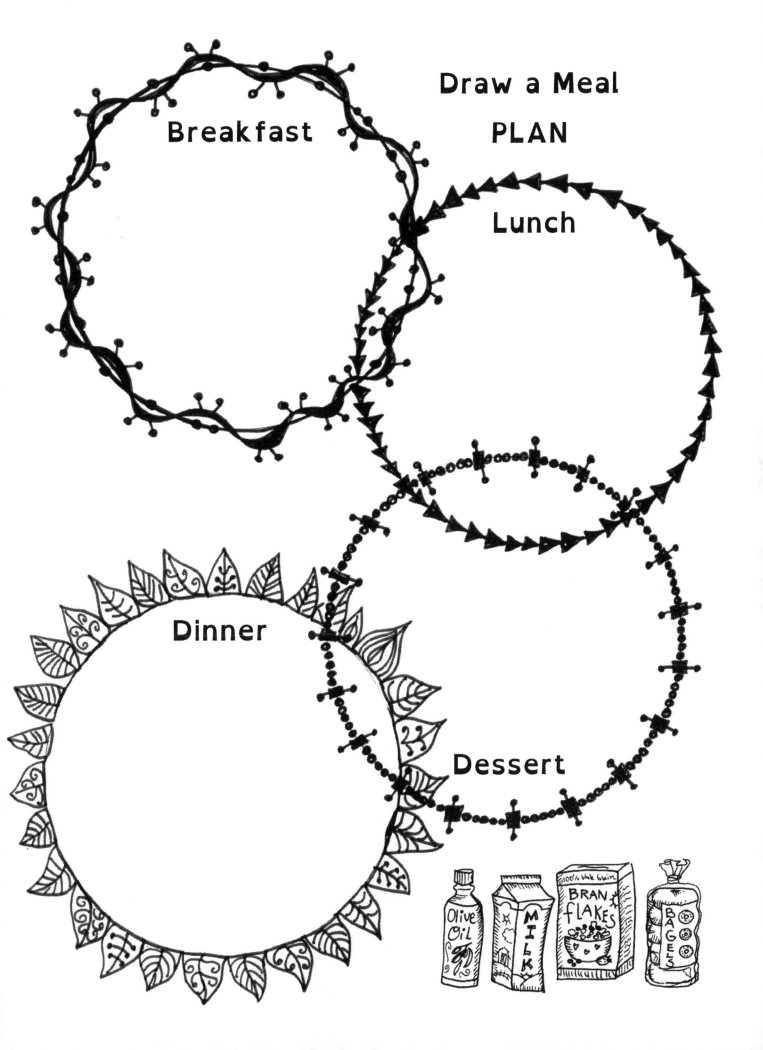

Breakfast

Draw a Meal
PLAN

Lunch

Dinner

Dessert

Reading Time - 1 Hour (Set a timer)

Choose TWO Books - Read from each book for 30 minutes.

Copy important words or pictures from your book here:

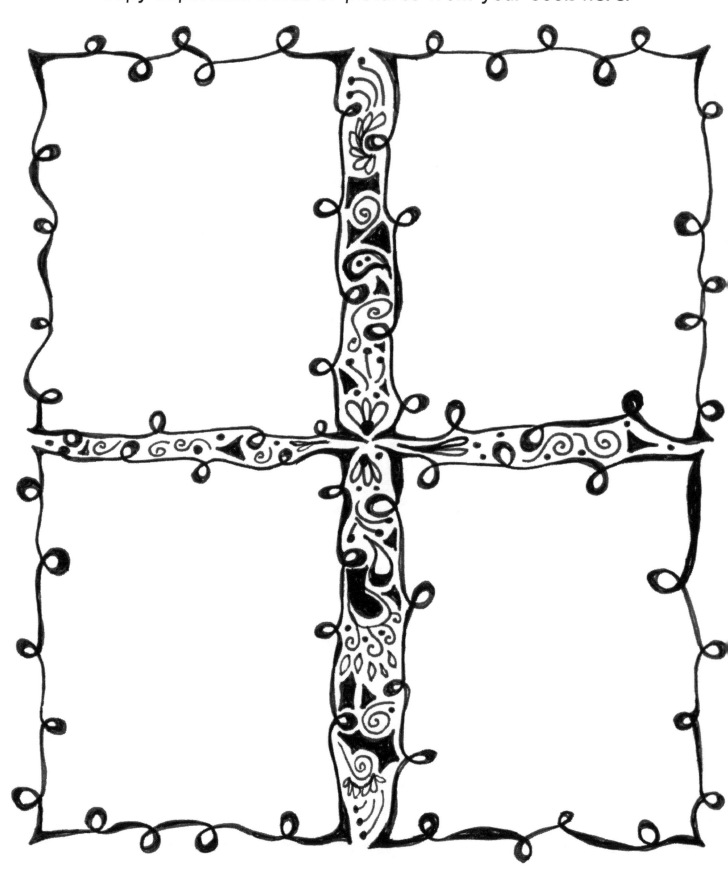

Spelling Time

Find 20 Words with **4** letters each.

Look in your books for words.

Write the words here:

DRAW A PICTURE
FROM ONE OF YOUR BOOKS:

COPYWORK

Find an interesting paragraph in one of your books and copy it. Be diligent to make your writing look exactly like it does in the book.

TITLE:_____

Page Number:_____

WRITE A STORY ABOUT THIS PICTURE

Circle Today's Date

January
February
March
April
May
June
July
August
September
October
November
December

1 2 3 4 5 6
7 8 9 10 11
12 13 14 15
16 17 18 19
20 21 22 23
24 25 26 27
28 29 30 31

MONDAY
TUESDAY
WEDNESDAY
THURSDAY
FRIDAY
SATURDAY
SUNDAY

2015
2016
2017
2018
2019
2020
2021
2022
2023
2024
2025
2026
2027
2028
2029

Write Today's Date:_____

Start Your Day!

Copy a Verse or Quote

_____

_____

_____

_____

_____

To-Do List

_____

_____

_____

_____

_____

_____

LEARN TO DRAW HORSES

Look at the Drawing.

Trace the Drawing

Draw the Missing Parts With a Smooth Black Pen.

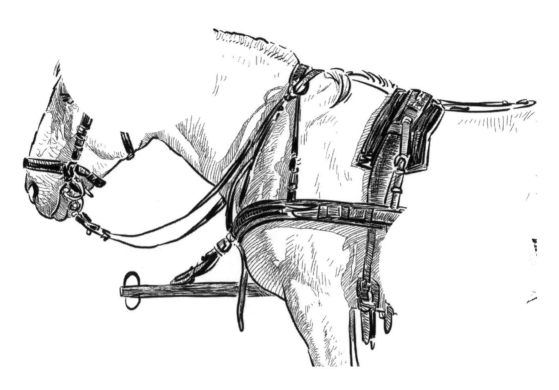

Draw it Yourself.

Reading Time - 1 Hour (Set a timer)

Choose TWO Books - Read from each book for 30 minutes.

Copy important words or pictures from your book here:

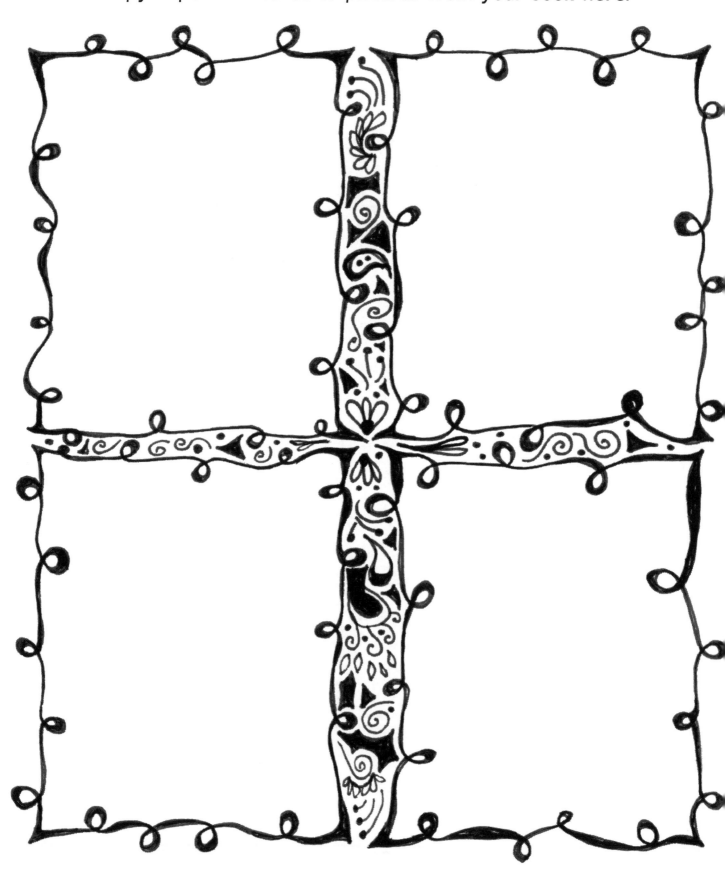

Fun With Letters! Just Add Color!

Hopes, Dreams & Ideas

USE YOUR COLORED PENCILS

Listening Time

Listen to an audio book or classical music or ask someone to read a story to you while you color and draw on the next page.

What are you listening to?

_____

Circle Today's Date

January
February
March
April
May
June
July
August
September
October
November
December

1 2 3 4 5 6
7 8 9 10 11
12 13 14 15
16 17 18 19
20 21 22 23
24 25 26 27
28 29 30 31

MONDAY
TUESDAY
WEDNESDAY
THURSDAY
FRIDAY
SATURDAY
SUNDAY

2015
2016
2017
2018
2019
2020
2021
2022
2023
2024
2025
2026
2027
2028
2029

Write Today's Date: _____

Start Your Day!

Copy a Verse or Quote

_____

_____

_____

_____

_____

To-Do List

_____

_____

_____

_____

_____

_____

Favorite Character:

_ _ _ _ _ _ _ _

Rate This Film:

1 2 3 4 5

Watch a Documentary, Or Movie about Horses.

TITLE:

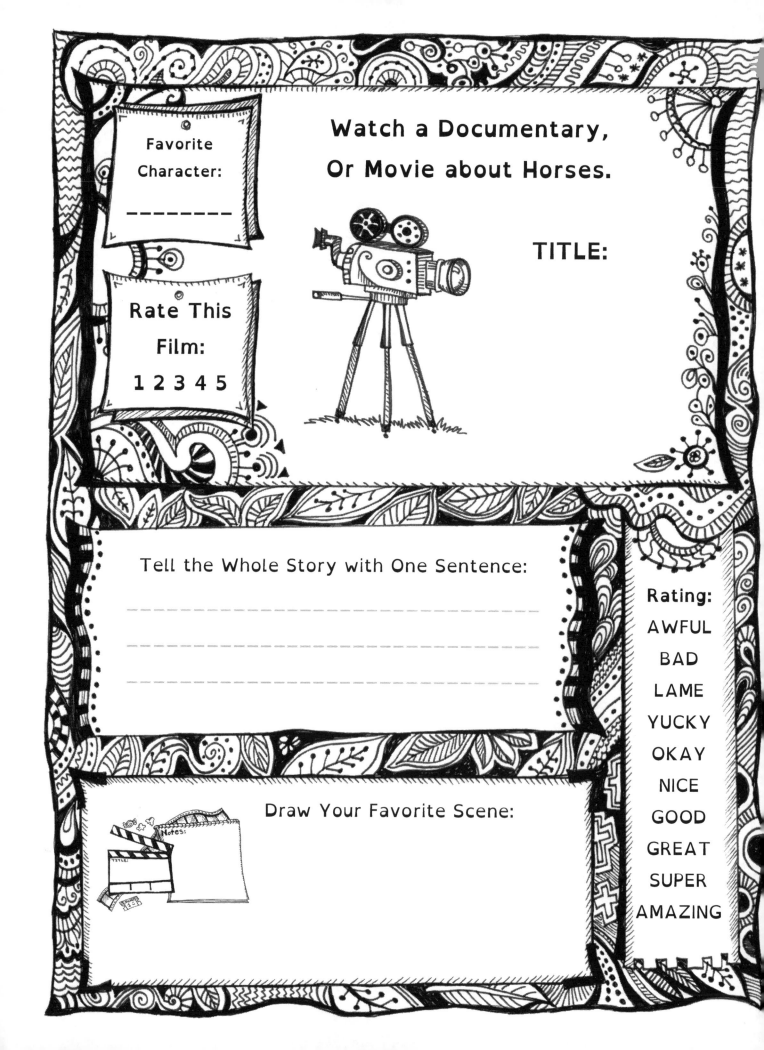

Tell the Whole Story with One Sentence:

Rating:

AWFUL

BAD

LAME

YUCKY

OKAY

NICE

GOOD

GREAT

SUPER

AMAZING

Draw Your Favorite Scene:

Notes:

USE YOUR COLORED PENCILS

Nature Study

Go outside and make a realistic
drawing of something
you find in nature.

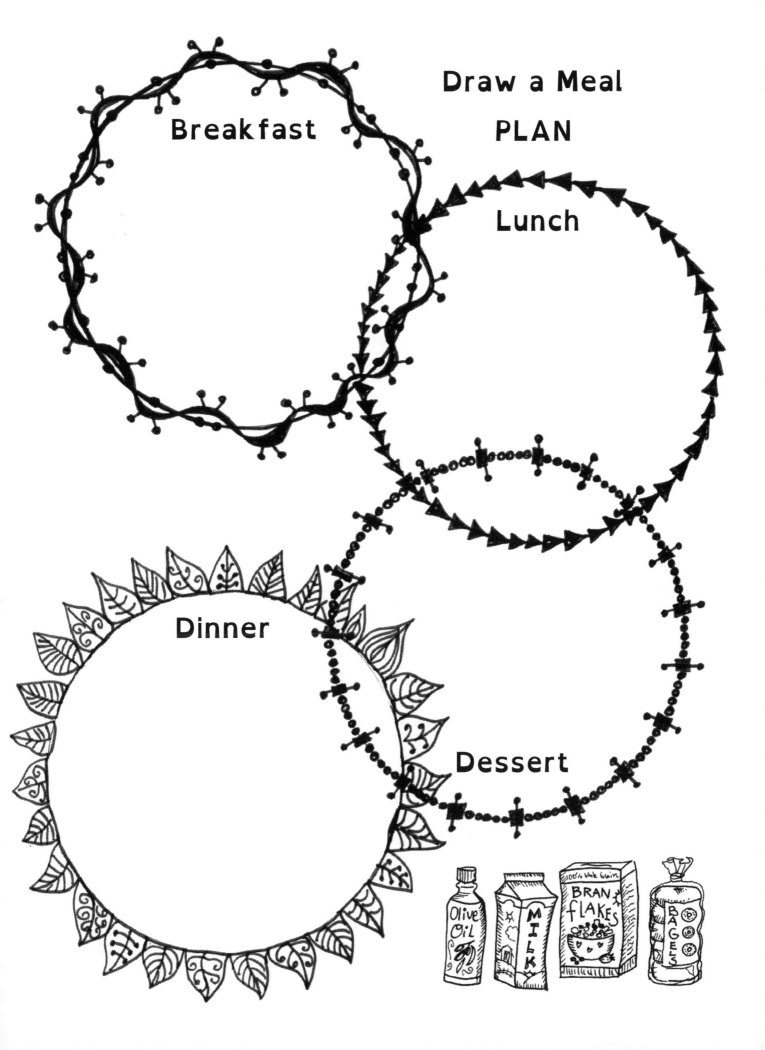

Reading Time - 1 Hour (Set a timer)

Choose TWO Books - Read from each book for 30 minutes.

Copy important words or pictures from your book here:

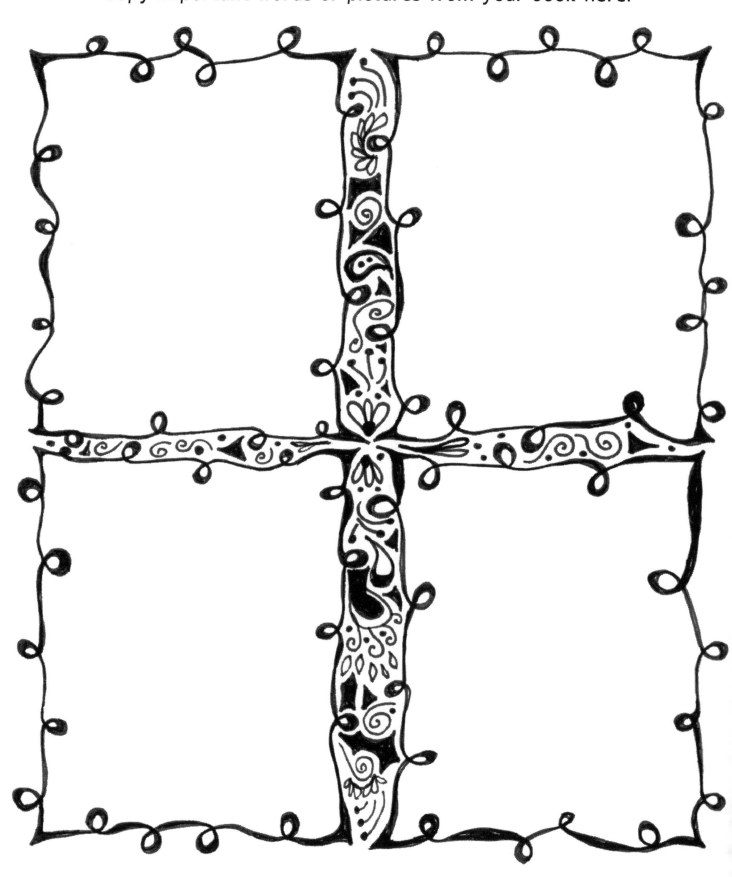

Spelling Time

Find 20 Words with **4** letters each.
Look in your books for words.
Write the words here:

_____   _____

_____   _____

_____   _____

_____   _____

_____   _____

_____   _____

_____   _____

_____   _____

_____   _____

COPYWORK

Find an interesting paragraph in one of your books and copy it. Be diligent to make your writing look exactly like it does in the book.

TITLE:_____

Page Number:_____

WRITE A STORY ABOUT THIS PICTURE

Circle Today's Date

January
February
March
April
May
June
July
August
September
October
November
December

1 2 3 4 5 6
7 8 9 10 11
12 13 14 15
16 17 18 19
20 21 22 23
24 25 26 27
28 29 30 31

MONDAY
TUESDAY
WEDNESDAY
THURSDAY
FRIDAY
SATURDAY
SUNDAY

2015
2016
2017
2018
2019
2020
2021
2022
2023
2024
2025
2026
2027
2028
2029

Write Today's Date: _____

Start Your Day!

Copy a Verse or Quote

_____

_____

_____

_____

_____

To-Do List

_____

_____

_____

_____

_____

_____

_____

LEARN TO DRAW HORSES

Draw the Missing Parts With a Smooth Black Pen.

Reading Time - 1 Hour (Set a timer)

Choose TWO Books - Read from each book for 30 minutes.

Copy important words or pictures from your book here:

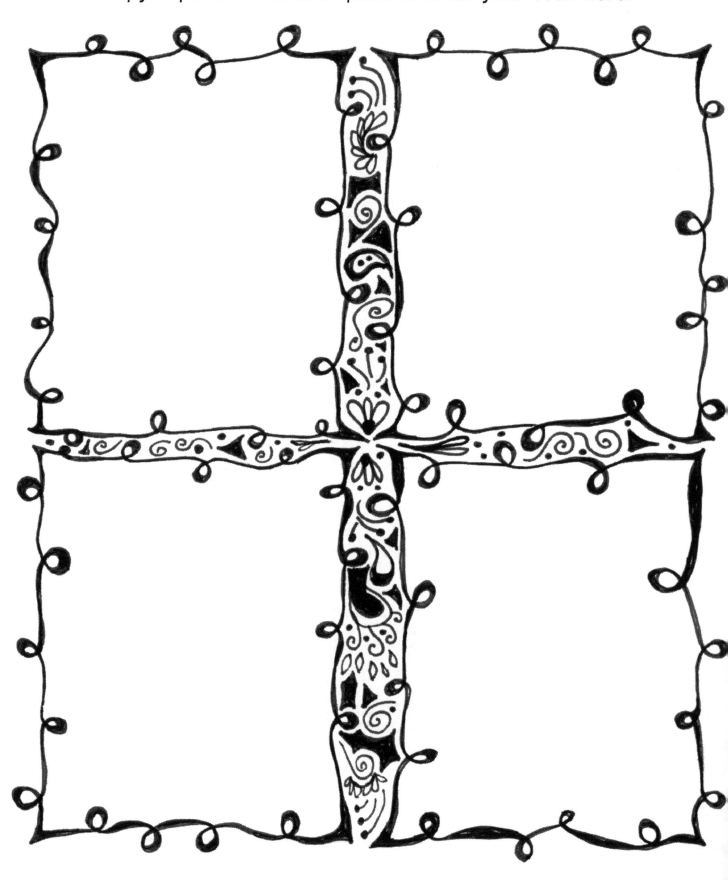

Fun With Letters! Just Add Color!

Hopes, Dreams & Ideas

USE YOUR COLORED PENCILS

Listening Time

Listen to an audio book or classical music or ask someone to read a story to you while you color and draw on the next page.

What are you listening to?

_____

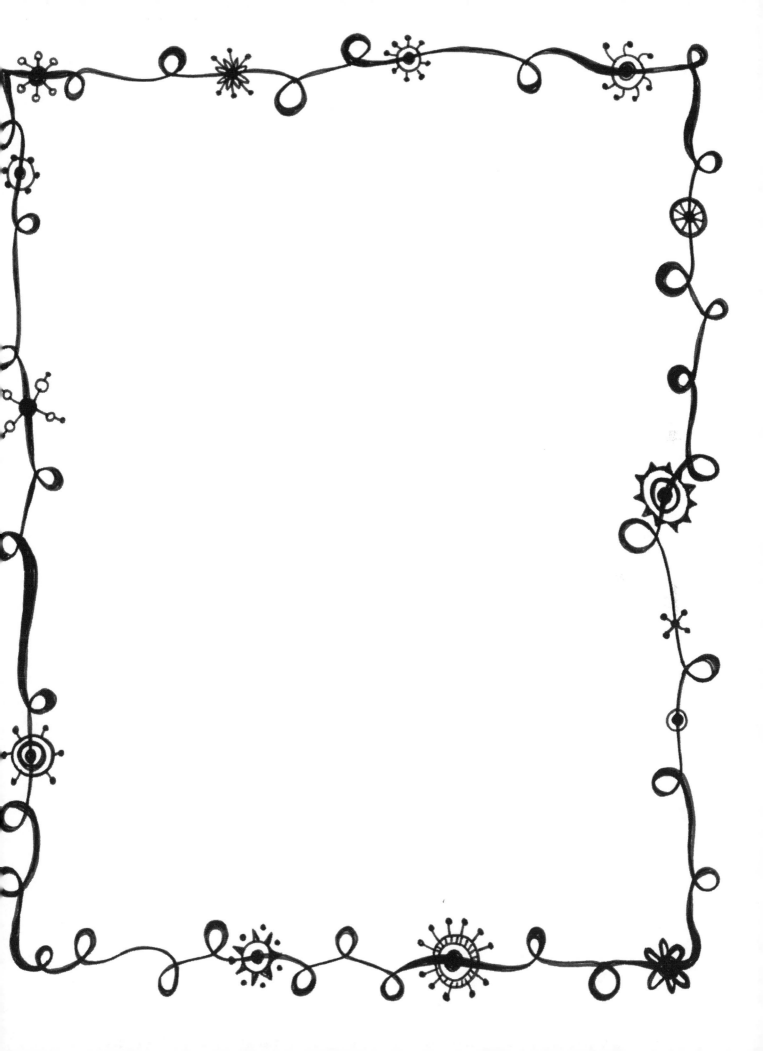

Circle Today's Date

January
February
March
April
May
June
July
August
September
October
November
December

1 2 3 4 5 6
7 8 9 10 11
12 13 14 15
16 17 18 19
20 21 22 23
24 25 26 27
28 29 30 31

MONDAY
TUESDAY
WEDNESDAY
THURSDAY
FRIDAY
SATURDAY
SUNDAY

2015
2016
2017
2018
2019
2020
2021
2022
2023
2024
2025
2026
2027
2028
2029

Write Today's Date: _____

Start Your Day!

Copy a Verse or Quote

_____

_____

_____

_____

_____

To-Do List

_____

_____

_____

_____

_____

_____

_____

Favorite Character:

————————

Watch a Documentary, Or Movie about Horses.

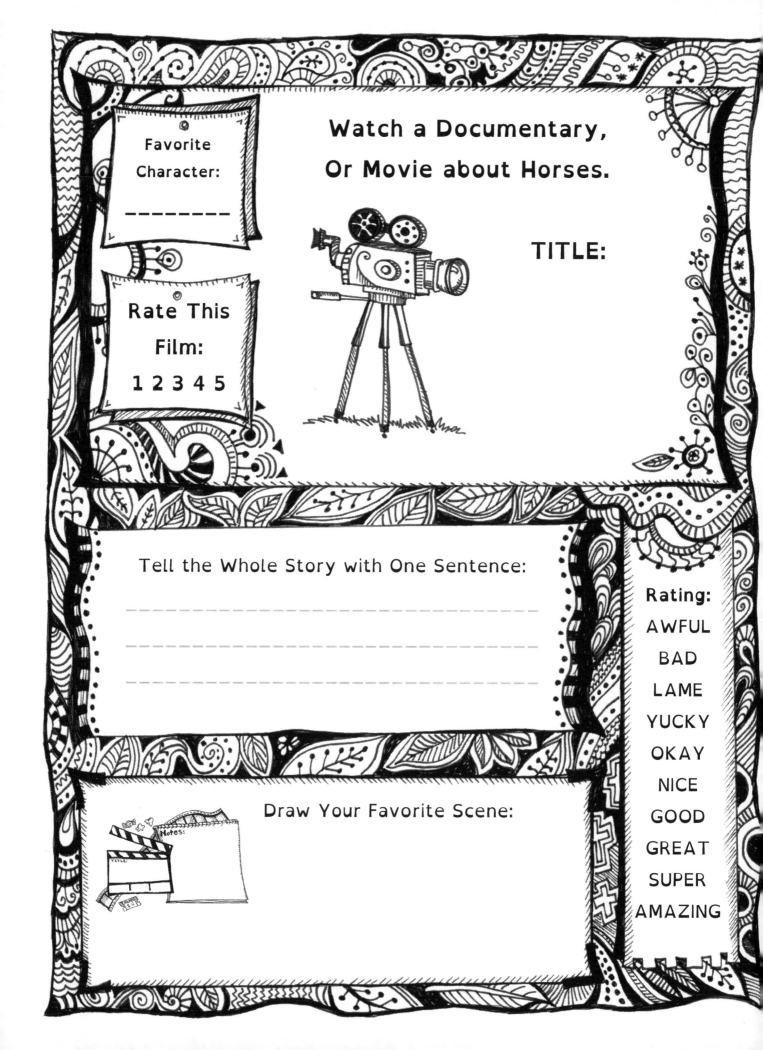

TITLE:

Rate This Film:

1 2 3 4 5

Tell the Whole Story with One Sentence:

Rating:

AWFUL

BAD

LAME

YUCKY

OKAY

NICE

GOOD

GREAT

SUPER

AMAZING

Draw Your Favorite Scene:

USE YOUR COLORED PENCILS

Nature Study

Go outside and make a realistic
drawing of something
you find in nature.

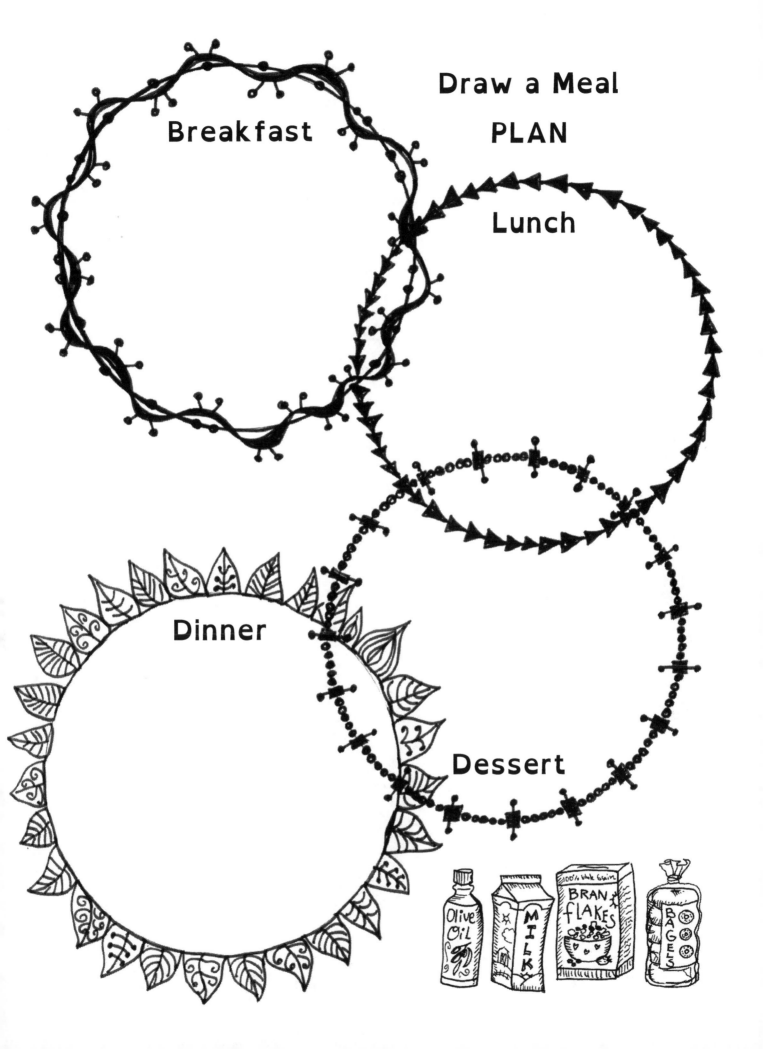

Reading Time - 1 Hour (Set a timer)

Choose TWO Books - Read from each book for 30 minutes.

Copy important words or pictures from your book here:

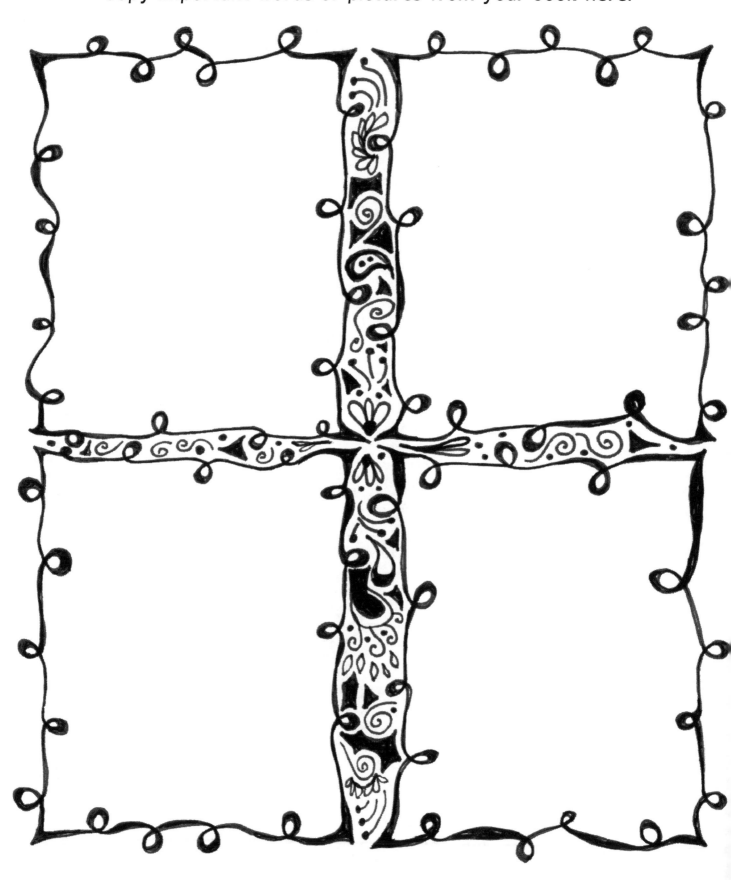

Spelling Time

Find 20 Words with **4** letters each.
Look in your books for words.
Write the words here:

_____ _____

_____ _____

_____ _____

_____ _____

_____ _____

_____ _____

_____ _____

_____ _____

_____ _____

_____ _____

DRAW A PICTURE FROM ONE OF YOUR BOOKS:

COPYWORK

Find an interesting paragraph in one of your books
and copy it. Be diligent to make your writing look
exactly like it does in the book.

TITLE:_____

Page Number:_____

WRITE A STORY ABOUT THIS PICTURE

Circle Today's Date

January
February
March
April
May
June
July
August
September
October
November
December

1 2 3 4 5 6
7 8 9 10 11
12 13 14 15
16 17 18 19
20 21 22 23
24 25 26 27
28 29 30 31

MONDAY
TUESDAY
WEDNESDAY
THURSDAY
FRIDAY
SATURDAY
SUNDAY

2015
2016
2017
2018
2019
2020
2021
2022
2023
2024
2025
2026
2027
2028
2029

Write Today's Date: _____

Start Your Day!

Copy a Verse or Quote

_ _

_ _

_ _

_ _

_ _

To-Do List

LEARN TO DRAW HORSES

Look at the Drawing.

Draw the Missing Parts With a Smooth Black Pen.

Reading Time - 1 Hour (Set a timer)

Choose TWO Books - Read from each book for 30 minutes.

Copy important words or pictures from your book here:

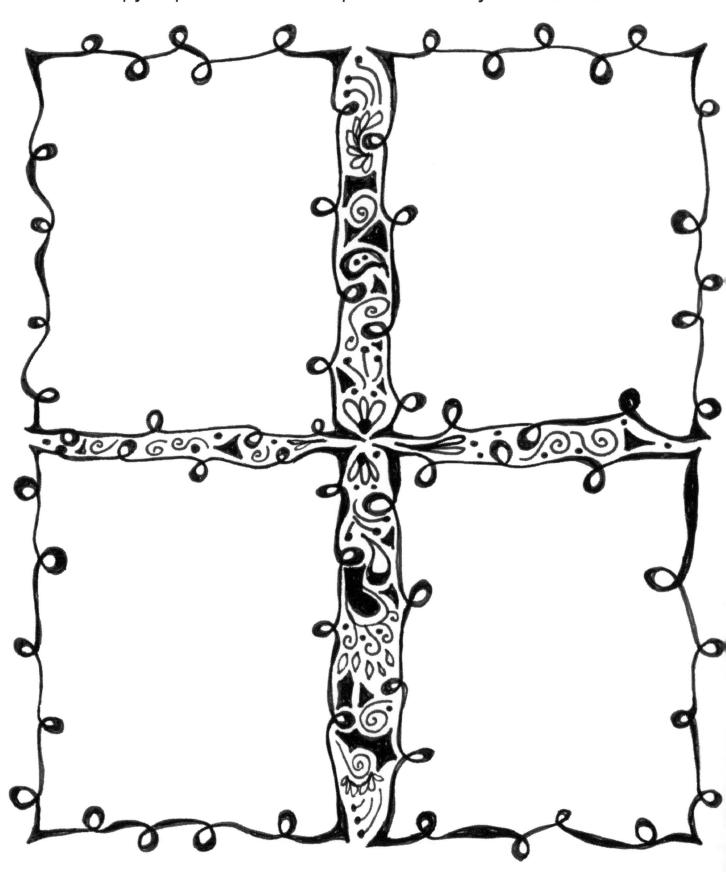

Spelling Time

Find 20 Words with **4** letters each.
Look in your books for words.
Write the words here:

_____   _____

_____   _____

_____   _____

_____   _____

_____   _____

_____   _____

_____   _____

_____   _____

_____   _____

_____   _____

Hopes, Dreams & Ideas

USE YOUR COLORED PENCILS

PRACTICE DRAWING HORSES

Circle Today's Date

January
February
March
April
May
June
July
August
September
October
November
December

1 2 3 4 5 6
7 8 9 10 11
12 13 14 15
16 17 18 19
20 21 22 23
24 25 26 27
28 29 30 31

MONDAY
TUESDAY
WEDNESDAY
THURSDAY
FRIDAY
SATURDAY
SUNDAY

2015
2016
2017
2018
2019
2020
2021
2022
2023
2024
2025
2026
2027
2028
2029

Write Today's Date: _____

Start Your Day!

Copy a Verse or Quote

_____

_____

_____

_____

_____

To-Do List

Favorite Character:

_____

Rate This Film:

1 2 3 4 5

Watch a Documentary, Or Movie about Horses.

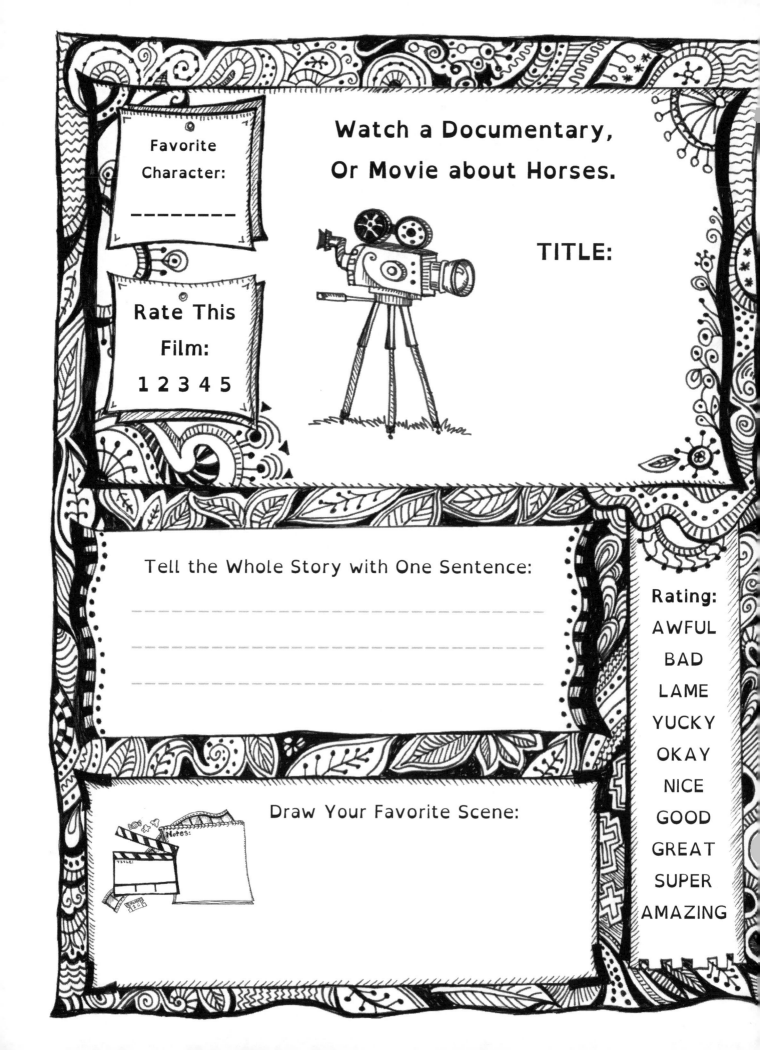

TITLE:

Tell the Whole Story with One Sentence:

Rating:

AWFUL

BAD

LAME

YUCKY

OKAY

NICE

GOOD

GREAT

SUPER

AMAZING

Draw Your Favorite Scene:

USE YOUR COLORED PENCILS

Nature Study

Go outside and make a realistic
drawing of something
you find in nature.

Fun With Letters! Just Add Color!

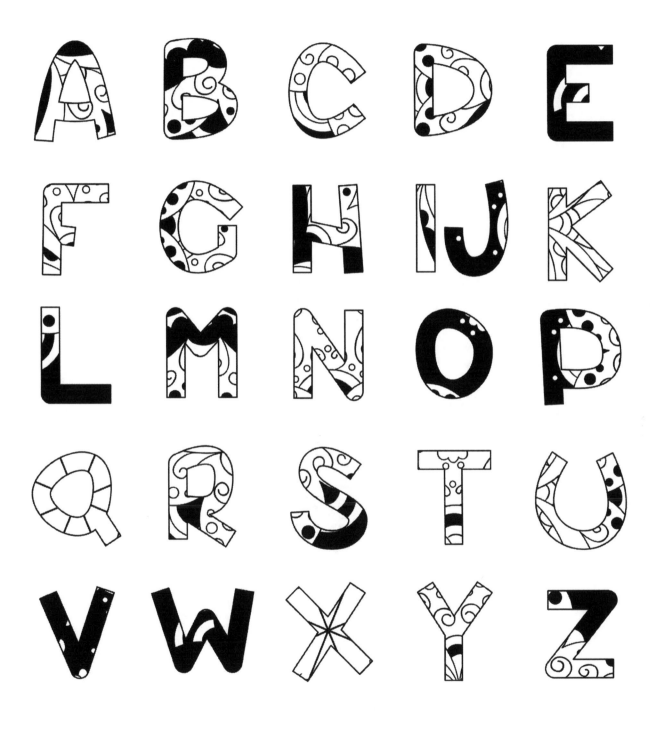

Reading Time - 1 Hour (Set a timer)
Choose TWO Books - Read from each book for 30 minutes.
Copy important words or pictures from your book here:

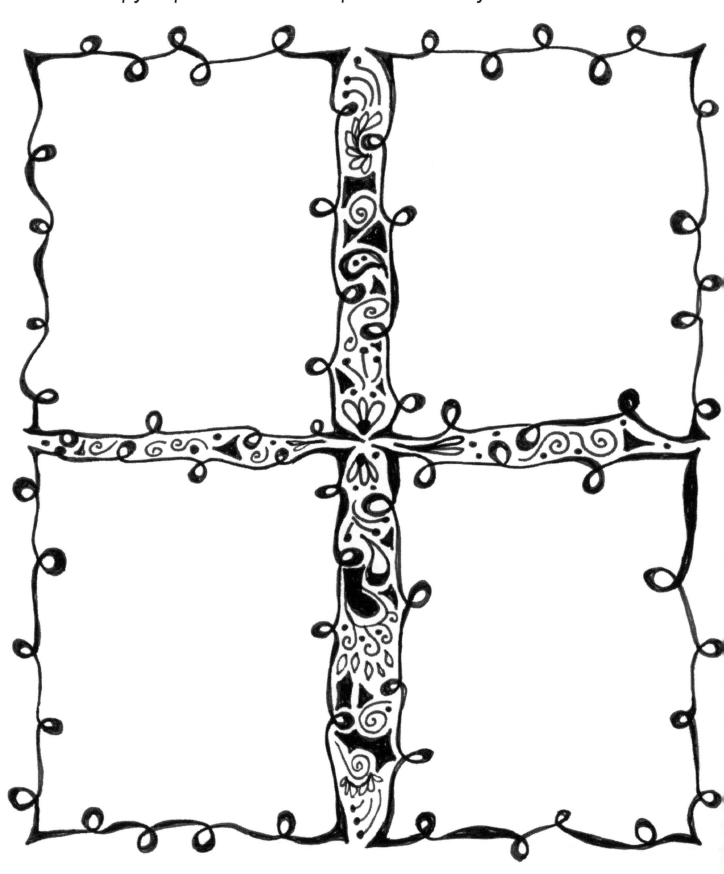

Spelling Time

Find 20 Words with 6 letters each.
Look in your books for words.
Write the words here:

_____   _____

_____   _____

_____   _____

_____   _____

_____   _____

_____   _____

_____   _____

_____   _____

_____   _____

DRAW A PICTURE
FROM ONE OF YOUR BOOKS:

COPYWORK

Find an interesting paragraph in one of your books and copy it. Be diligent to make your writing look exactly like it does in the book.

TITLE:_____

Page Number:_____

WRITE A STORY ABOUT THIS PICTURE

Circle Today's Date

January
February
March
April
May
June
July
August
September
October
November
December

1 2 3 4 5 6
7 8 9 10 11
12 13 14 15
16 17 18 19
20 21 22 23
24 25 26 27
28 29 30 31

MONDAY
TUESDAY
WEDNESDAY
THURSDAY
FRIDAY
SATURDAY
SUNDAY

2015
2016
2017
2018
2019
2020
2021
2022
2023
2024
2025
2026
2027
2028
2029

Write Today's Date: _____

Start Your Day!

Copy a Verse or Quote

_____

_____

_____

_____

_____

To-Do List

_____

_____

_____

_____

_____

_____

LEARN TO DRAW HORSES

Look at the Drawing.

Draw the Missing Parts With a Smooth Black Pen.

Reading Time - 1 Hour (Set a timer)

Choose TWO Books - Read from each book for 30 minutes.

Copy important words or pictures from your book here:

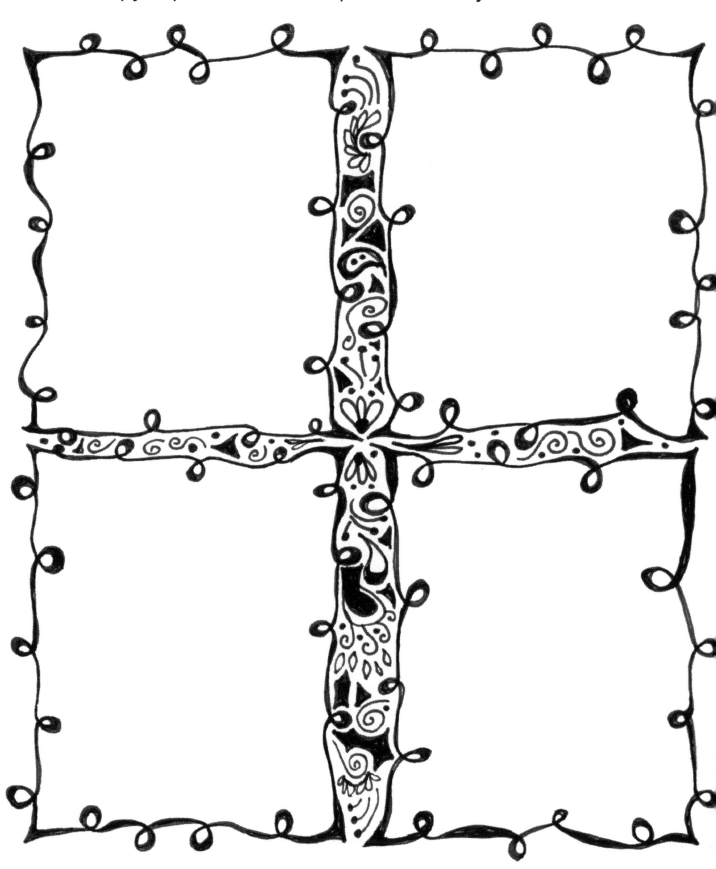

Spelling Time

Find 20 Words with **7** letters each.

Look in your books for words.

Write the words here:

_____   _____

_____   _____

_____   _____

_____   _____

_____   _____

_____   _____

_____   _____

_____   _____

_____   _____

Hopes, Dreams & Ideas

USE YOUR COLORED PENCILS

PRACTICE DRAWING HORSES

Circle Today's Date

January	1 2 3 4 5 6
February	7 8 9 10 11
March	12 13 14 15
April	16 17 18 19
May	20 21 22 23
June	24 25 26 27
July	28 29 30 31
August	
September	
October	
November	
December	

MONDAY
TUESDAY
WEDNESDAY
THURSDAY
FRIDAY
SATURDAY
SUNDAY

2015
2016
2017
2018
2019
2020
2021
2022
2023
2024
2025
2026
2027
2028
2029

Write Today's Date: _ _ _ _ _ _ _ _ _ _ _ _ _ _ _ _

Start Your Day!

Copy a Verse or Quote

_____

_____

_____

_____

_____

To-Do List

_____
_____
_____
_____
_____
_____

Favorite Character:

_____

Watch a Documentary, Or Movie about Horses.

TITLE:

Rate This Film:

1 2 3 4 5

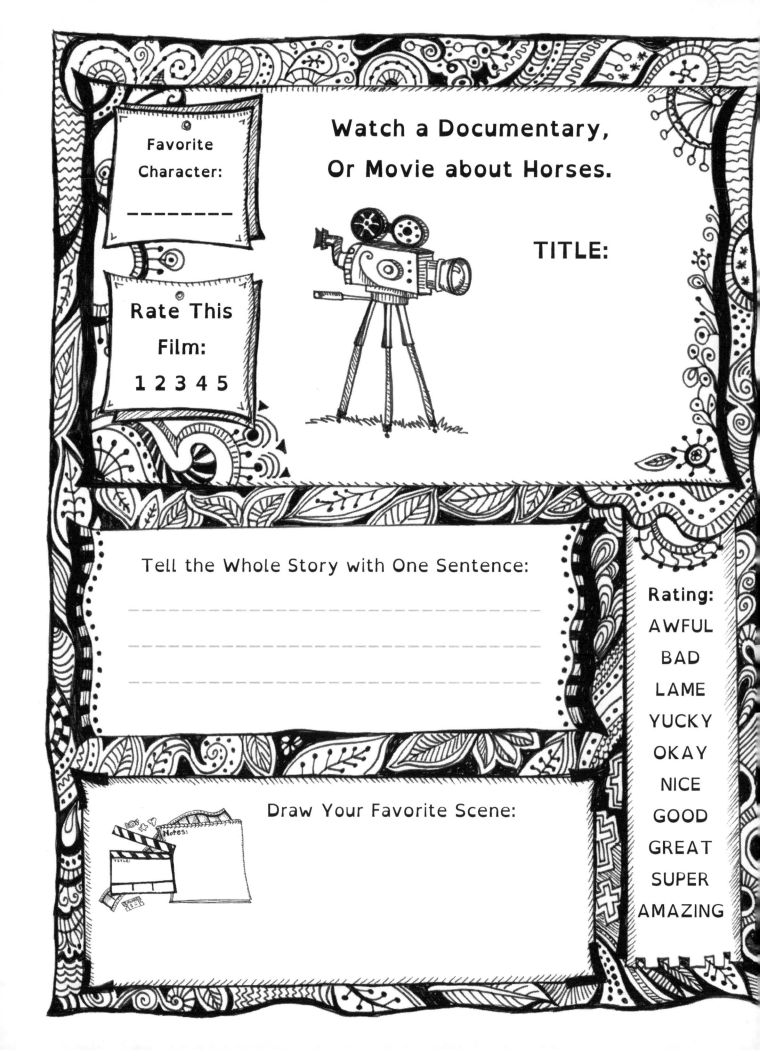

Tell the Whole Story with One Sentence:

_____
_____
_____

Rating:

AWFUL

BAD

LAME

YUCKY

OKAY

NICE

GOOD

GREAT

SUPER

AMAZING

Notes:

Draw Your Favorite Scene:

USE YOUR COLORED PENCILS

Nature Study

Go outside and make a realistic
drawing of something
you find in nature.

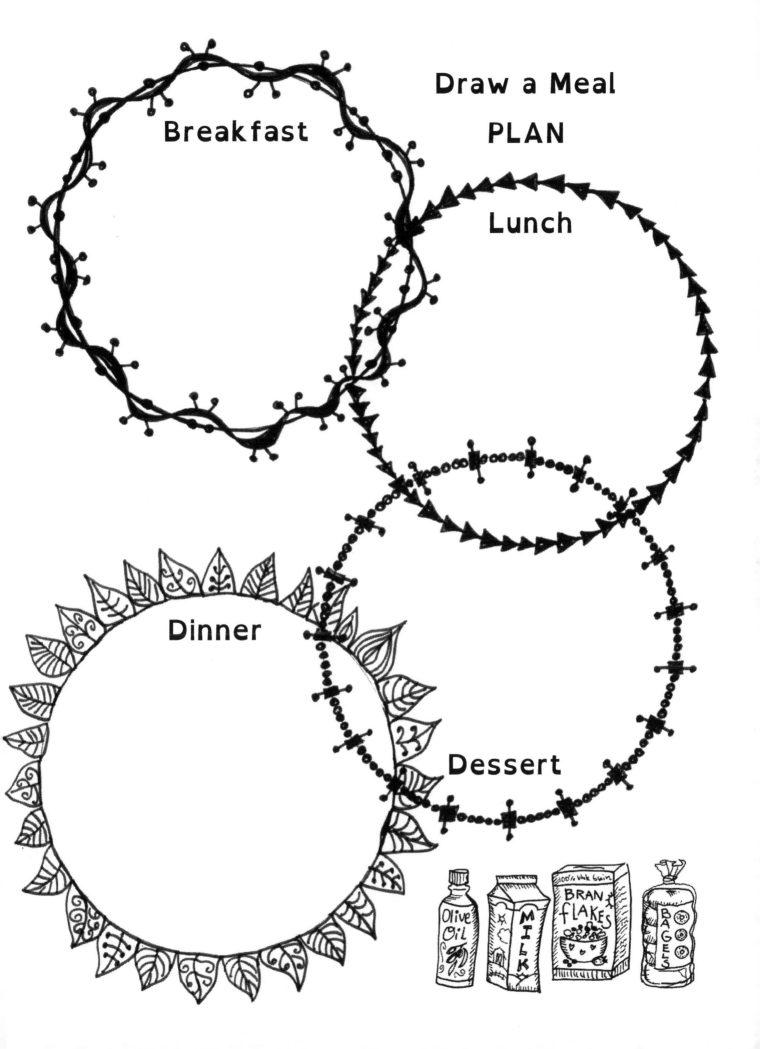

Draw a Meal
PLAN

Breakfast

Lunch

Dinner

Dessert

Reading Time - 1 Hour (Set a timer)

Choose TWO Books - Read from each book for 30 minutes.

Copy important words or pictures from your book here:

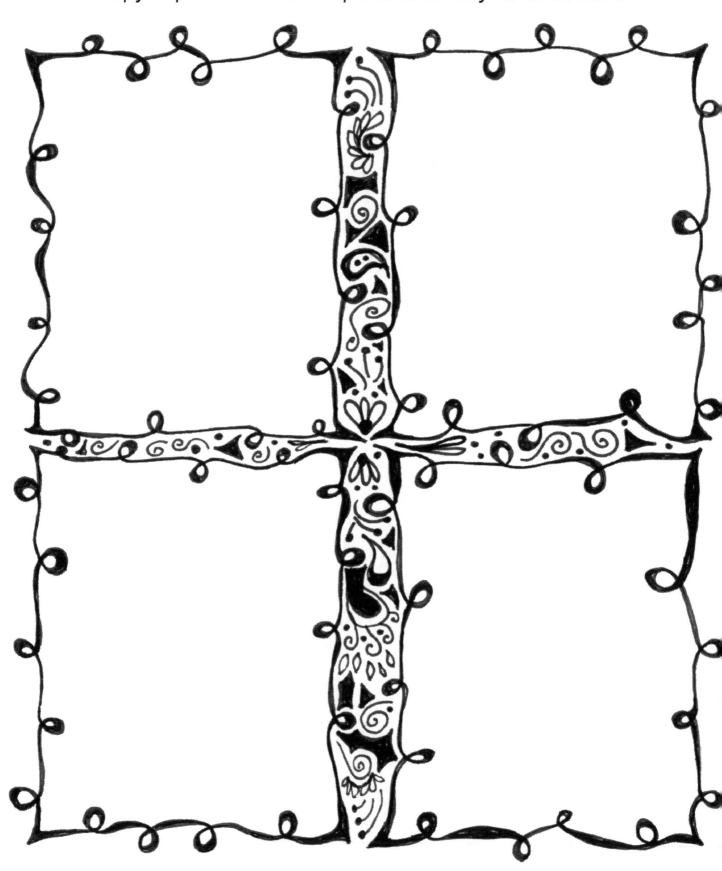

Spelling Time

Find 20 Words with **4** letters each.

Look in your books for words.

Write the words here:

DRAW A PICTURE
FROM ONE OF YOUR BOOKS:

COPYWORK

Find an interesting paragraph in one of your books and copy it. Be diligent to make your writing look exactly like it does in the book.

TITLE:_____

Page Number:_____

WRITE A STORY ABOUT THIS PICTURE

Listening Time

Listen to an audio book or classical music or
ask someone to read a story to you while
you color and draw on the next page.

What are you listening to?

_____

Circle Today's Date

January
February
March
April
May
June
July
August
September
October
November
December

1 2 3 4 5 6
7 8 9 10 11
12 13 14 15
16 17 18 19
20 21 22 23
24 25 26 27
28 29 30 31

MONDAY
TUESDAY
WEDNESDAY
THURSDAY
FRIDAY
SATURDAY
SUNDAY

2015
2016
2017
2018
2019
2020
2021
2022
2023
2024
2025
2026
2027
2028
2029

Write Today's Date: _ _ _ _ _ _ _ _ _ _ _ _ _ _ _ _

Start Your Day!

Copy a Verse or Quote

_____

_____

_____

_____

_____

To-Do List

_____

_____

_____

_____

_____

_____

LEARN TO DRAW HORSES

Look at the Drawing.

Draw the Missing Parts With a Smooth Black Pen.

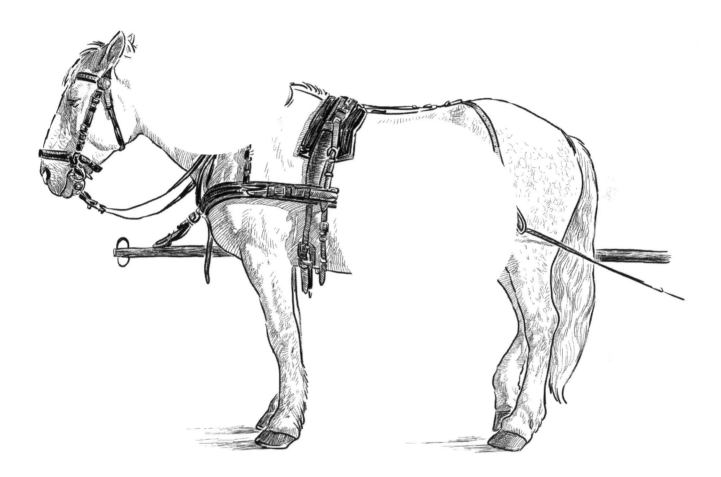

Reading Time - 1 Hour (Set a timer)

Choose TWO Books - Read from each book for 30 minutes.

Copy important words or pictures from your book here:

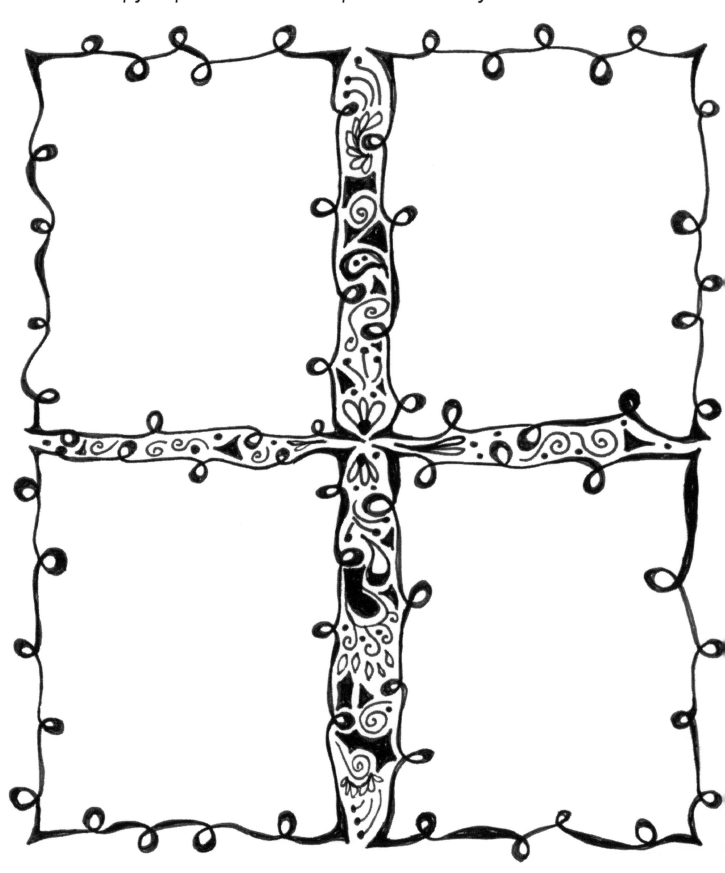

Fun With Letters! Just Add Color!

A B C D E F G
H I J K L M N
O P Q R S T U
V W X Y Z
1 2 3 4 5 6 7 8 9 0

Hopes, Dreams & Ideas

USE YOUR COLORED PENCILS

PRACTICE DRAWING HORSES

Circle Today's Date

January
February
March
April
May
June
July
August
September
October
November
December

1 2 3 4 5 6
7 8 9 10 11
12 13 14 15
16 17 18 19
20 21 22 23
24 25 26 27
28 29 30 31

MONDAY
TUESDAY
WEDNESDAY
THURSDAY
FRIDAY
SATURDAY
SUNDAY

2015
2016
2017
2018
2019
2020
2021
2022
2023
2024
2025
2026
2027
2028
2029

Write Today's Date: _ _ _ _ _ _ _ _ _ _ _ _ _ _ _ _

Start Your Day!

Copy a Verse or Quote

_____

_____

_____

_____

_____

To-Do List

_____

_____

_____

_____

_____

_____

Favorite
Character:

_ _ _ _ _ _ _

Watch a Documentary,
Or Movie about Horses.

TITLE:

Rate This
Film:

1 2 3 4 5

Tell the Whole Story with One Sentence:

Rating:

AWFUL

BAD

LAME

YUCKY

OKAY

NICE

GOOD

GREAT

SUPER

AMAZING

Draw Your Favorite Scene:

USE YOUR COLORED PENCILS

Nature Study

Go outside and make a realistic
drawing of something
you find in nature.

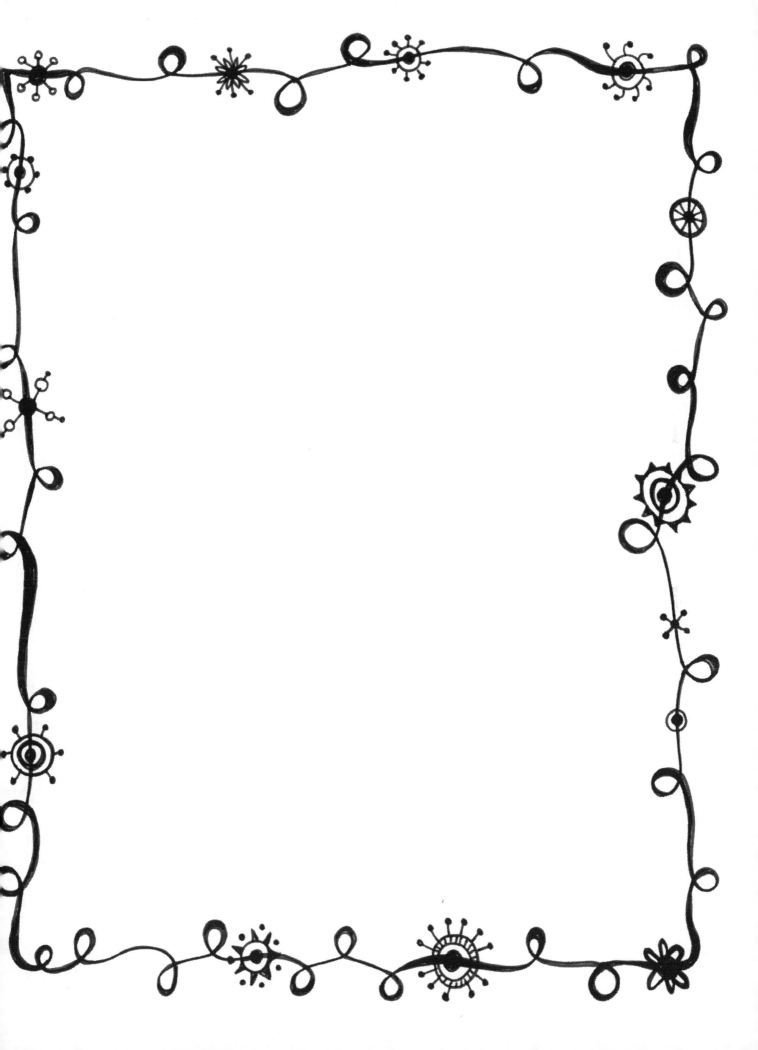

Reading Time - 1 Hour (Set a timer)

Choose TWO Books - Read from each book for 30 minutes.
Copy important words or pictures from your book here:

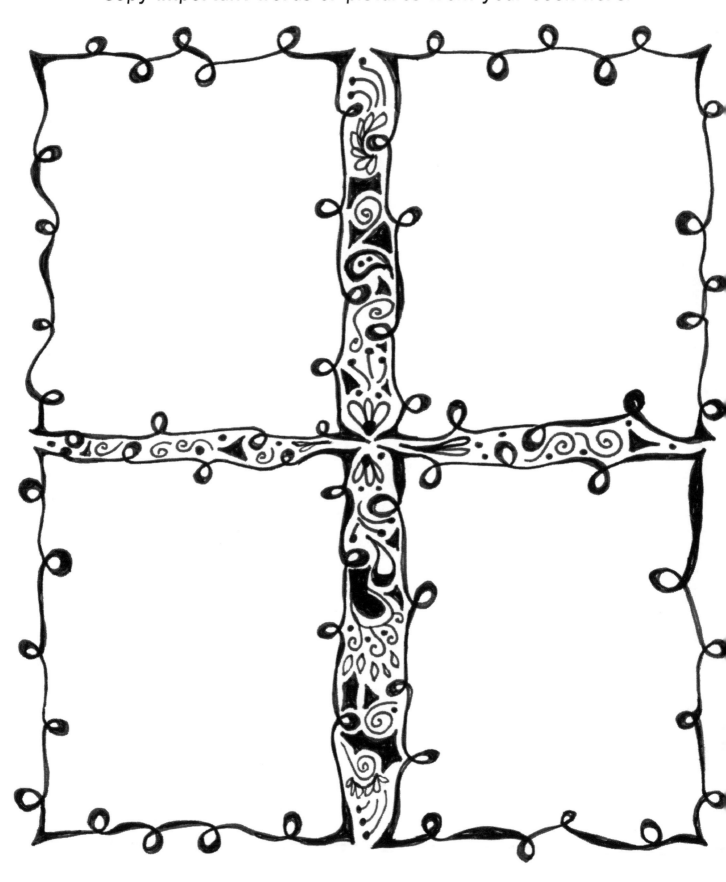

Spelling Time

Find 20 Words with 4 letters each.
Look in your books for words.
Write the words here:

DRAW A PICTURE
FROM ONE OF YOUR BOOKS:

COPYWORK

Find an interesting paragraph in one of your books and copy it. Be diligent to make your writing look exactly like it does in the book.

TITLE:_____

Page Number:_____

WRITE A STORY ABOUT THIS PICTURE

Circle Today's Date

January
February
March
April
May
June
July
August
September
October
November
December

1 2 3 4 5 6
7 8 9 10 11
12 13 14 15
16 17 18 19
20 21 22 23
24 25 26 27
28 29 30 31

MONDAY
TUESDAY
WEDNESDAY
THURSDAY
FRIDAY
SATURDAY
SUNDAY

2015
2016
2017
2018
2019
2020
2021
2022
2023
2024
2025
2026
2027
2028
2029

Write Today's Date: _ _ _ _ _ _ _ _ _ _ _ _ _ _ _

Start Your Day!

Copy a Verse or Quote

— — — — — — — — — — — — — — —

— — — — — — — — — — — — — — —

— — — — — — — — — — — — — — —

— — — — — — — — — — — — — — —

— — — — — — — — — — — — — — —

To-Do List

LEARN TO DRAW HORSES

Look at the Drawing.

Draw the Missing Parts With a Smooth Black Pen.

Reading Time - 1 Hour (Set a timer)

Choose TWO Books - Read from each book for 30 minutes.

Copy important words or pictures from your book here:

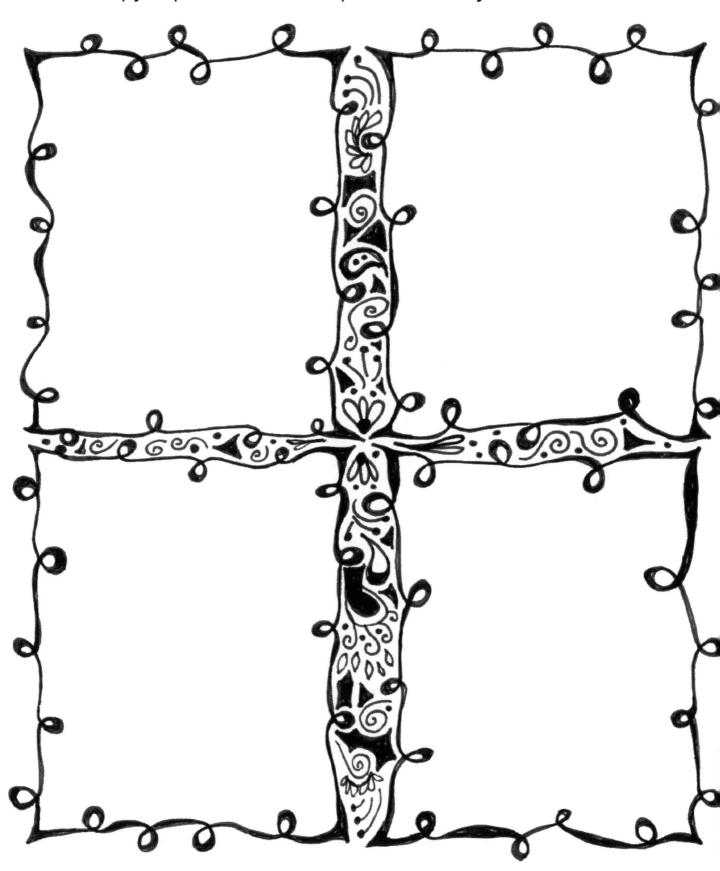

Spelling Time

Find 20 Words with **8** letters each.

Look in your books for words.

Write the words here:

_____   _____

_____   _____

_____   _____

_____   _____

_____   _____

_____   _____

_____   _____

_____   _____

_____   _____

Hopes, Dreams & Ideas

USE YOUR COLORED PENCILS

PRACTICE DRAWING HORSES

Circle Today's Date

January
February
March
April
May
June
July
August
September
October
November
December

1 2 3 4 5 6
7 8 9 10 11
12 13 14 15
16 17 18 19
20 21 22 23
24 25 26 27
28 29 30 31

MONDAY
TUESDAY
WEDNESDAY
THURSDAY
FRIDAY
SATURDAY
SUNDAY

2015
2016
2017
2018
2019
2020
2021
2022
2023
2024
2025
2026
2027
2028
2029

Write Today's Date: _ _ _ _ _ _ _ _ _ _ _ _ _ _

Start Your Day!

Copy a Verse or Quote

— — — — — — — — — — — — — — —

— — — — — — — — — — — — — — —

— — — — — — — — — — — — — — —

— — — — — — — — — — — — — — —

— — — — — — — — — — — — — — —

To-Do List

_____

_____

_____

_____

_____

_____

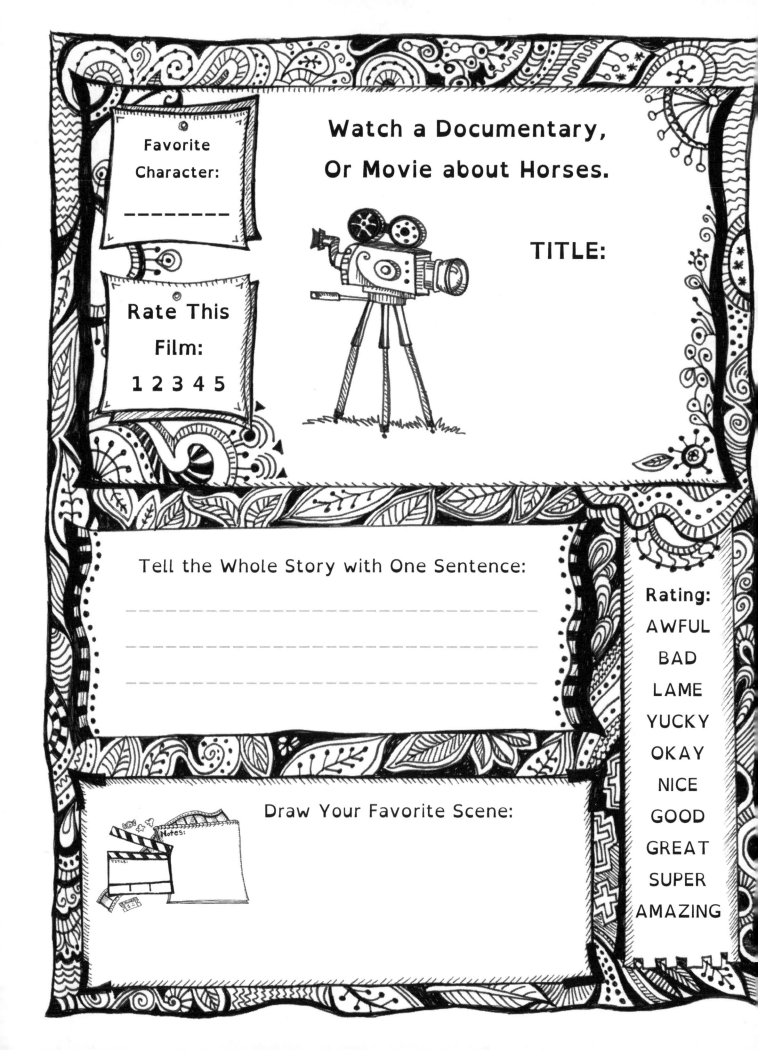

Favorite Character:

_ _ _ _ _ _ _ _

Rate This Film:

1 2 3 4 5

Watch a Documentary, Or Movie about Horses.

TITLE:

Tell the Whole Story with One Sentence:

Draw Your Favorite Scene:

Rating:

AWFUL

BAD

LAME

YUCKY

OKAY

NICE

GOOD

GREAT

SUPER

AMAZING

USE YOUR COLORED PENCILS

Nature Study

Go outside and make a realistic
drawing of something
you find in nature.

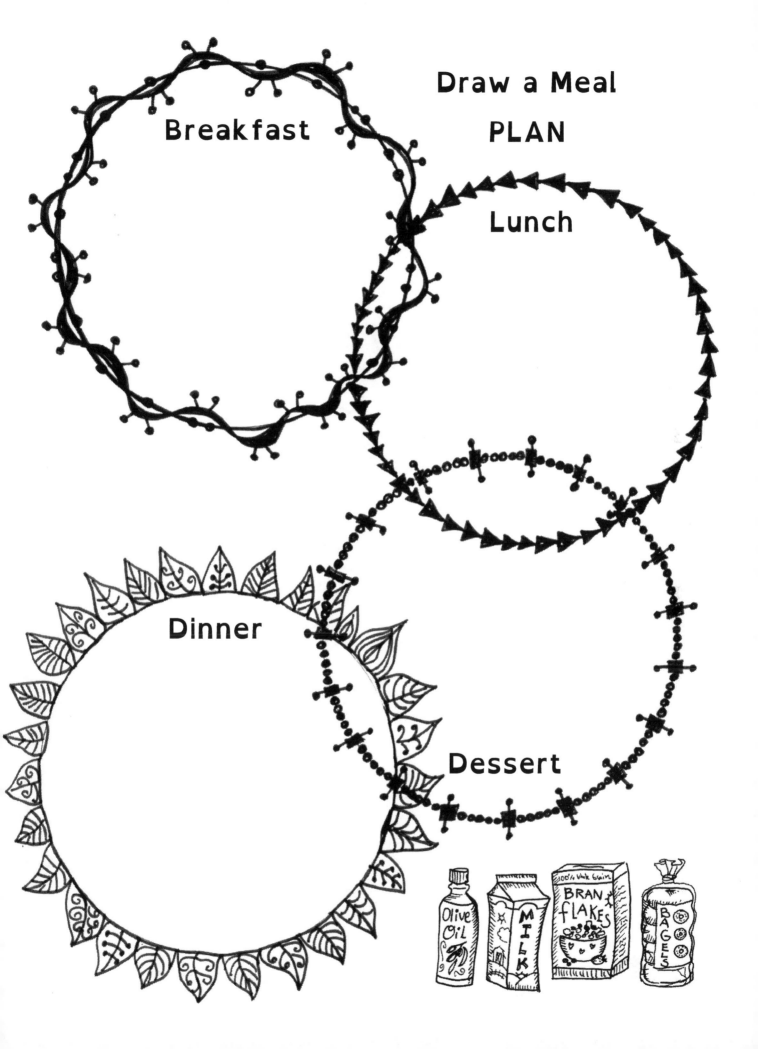

Draw a Meal PLAN

Breakfast

Lunch

Dinner

Dessert

Reading Time - 1 Hour (Set a timer)

Choose TWO Books - Read from each book for 30 minutes.

Copy important words or pictures from your book here:

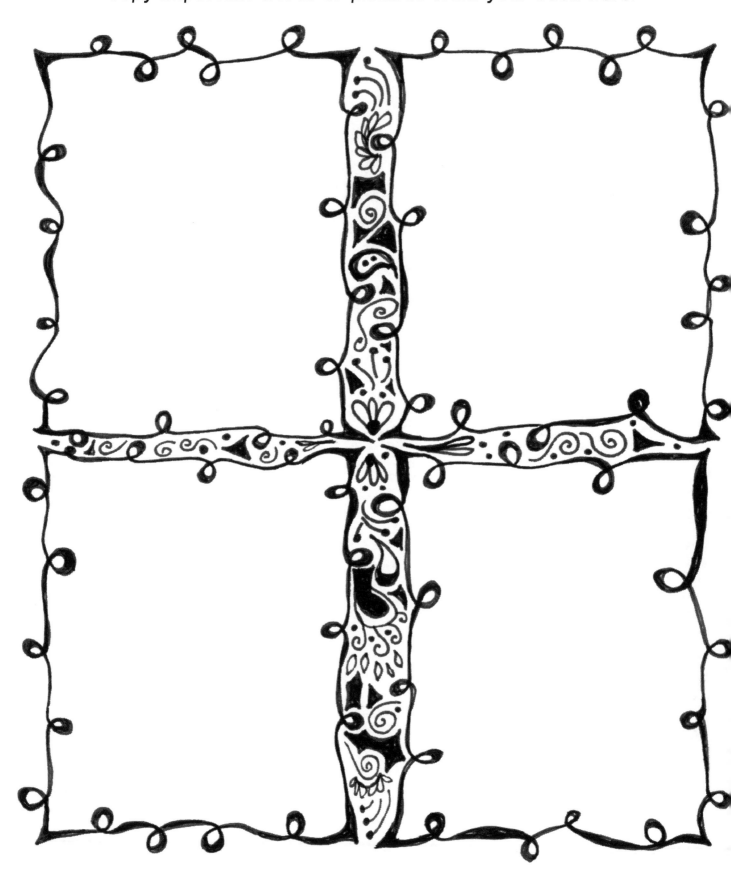

Spelling Time

Find 20 Words with **4** letters each.
Look in your books for words.
Write the words here:

_____   _____

_____   _____

_____   _____

_____   _____

_____   _____

_____   _____

_____   _____

_____   _____

_____   _____

DRAW A PICTURE
FROM ONE OF YOUR BOOKS:

COPYWORK

Find an interesting paragraph in one of your books and copy it. Be diligent to make your writing look exactly like it does in the book.

TITLE:_____

Page Number:_____

WRITE A STORY ABOUT THIS PICTURE

Circle Today's Date

January
February
March
April
May
June
July
August
September
October
November
December

1 2 3 4 5 6
7 8 9 10 11
12 13 14 15
16 17 18 19
20 21 22 23
24 25 26 27
28 29 30 31

MONDAY
TUESDAY
WEDNESDAY
THURSDAY
FRIDAY
SATURDAY
SUNDAY

2015
2016
2017
2018
2019
2020
2021
2022
2023
2024
2025
2026
2027
2028
2029

Write Today's Date: _ _ _ _ _ _ _ _ _ _ _ _ _ _ _ _ _

Start Your Day!

Copy a Verse or Quote

_____

_____

_____

_____

_____

To-Do List

_____

_____

_____

_____

_____

_____

LEARN TO DRAW HORSES

Look at the Drawing.

Draw the Missing Parts With a Smooth Black Pen.

Reading Time - 1 Hour (Set a timer)

Choose TWO Books - Read from each book for 30 minutes.

Copy important words or pictures from your book here:

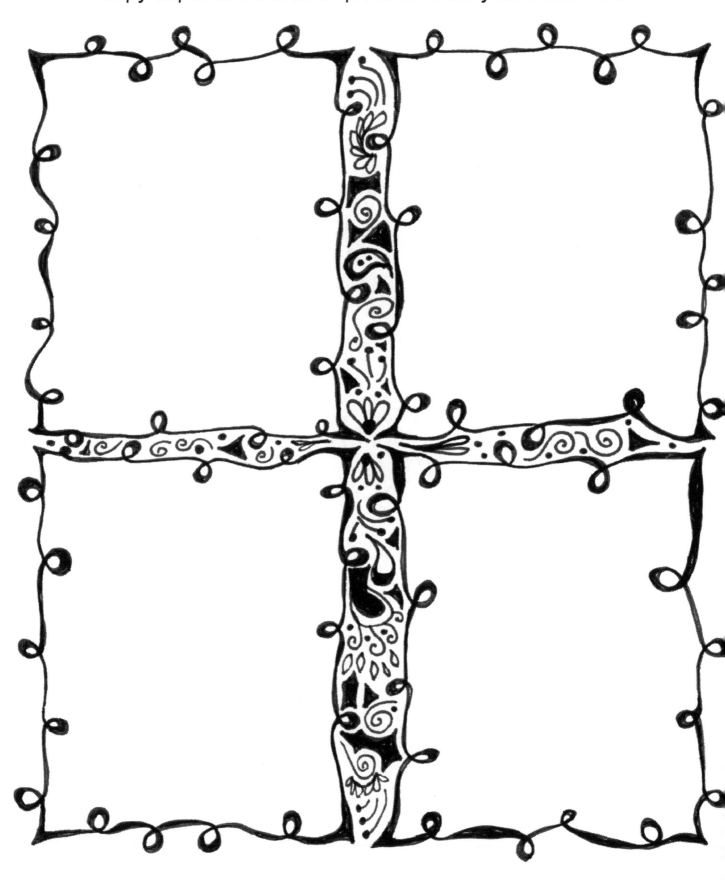

Spelling Time

Find 20 Words with **4** letters each.
Look in your books for words.
Write the words here:

_____   _____

_____   _____

_____   _____

_____   _____

_____   _____

_____   _____

_____   _____

_____   _____

_____   _____

_____   _____

Hopes, Dreams & Ideas

USE YOUR COLORED PENCILS

PRACTICE DRAWING HORSES

Circle Today's Date

January
February
March
April
May
June
July
August
September
October
November
December

1 2 3 4 5 6
7 8 9 10 11
12 13 14 15
16 17 18 19
20 21 22 23
24 25 26 27
28 29 30 31

MONDAY
TUESDAY
WEDNESDAY
THURSDAY
FRIDAY
SATURDAY
SUNDAY

2015
2016
2017
2018
2019
2020
2021
2022
2023
2024
2025
2026
2027
2028
2029

Write Today's Date: _ _ _ _ _ _ _ _ _ _ _ _ _ _ _ _

Start Your Day!

Copy a Verse or Quote

_____

_____

_____

_____

_____

To-Do List

_____

_____

_____

_____

_____

_____

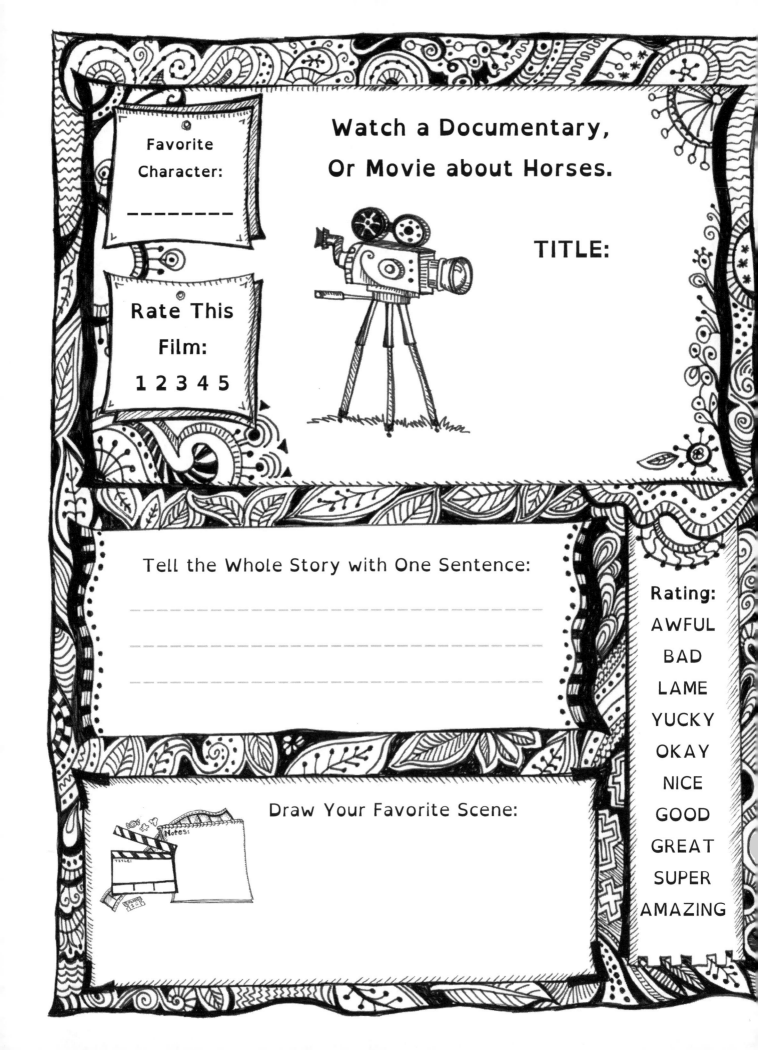

Favorite Character:

_____

Rate This Film:

1 2 3 4 5

Watch a Documentary, Or Movie about Horses.

TITLE:

Tell the Whole Story with One Sentence:

Draw Your Favorite Scene:

Notes:

Rating:

AWFUL

BAD

LAME

YUCKY

OKAY

NICE

GOOD

GREAT

SUPER

AMAZING

Nature Study

Go outside and make a realistic
drawing of something
you find in nature.

Fun With Letters! Just Add Color!

Reading Time - 1 Hour (Set a timer)

Choose TWO Books - Read from each book for 30 minutes.

Copy important words or pictures from your book here:

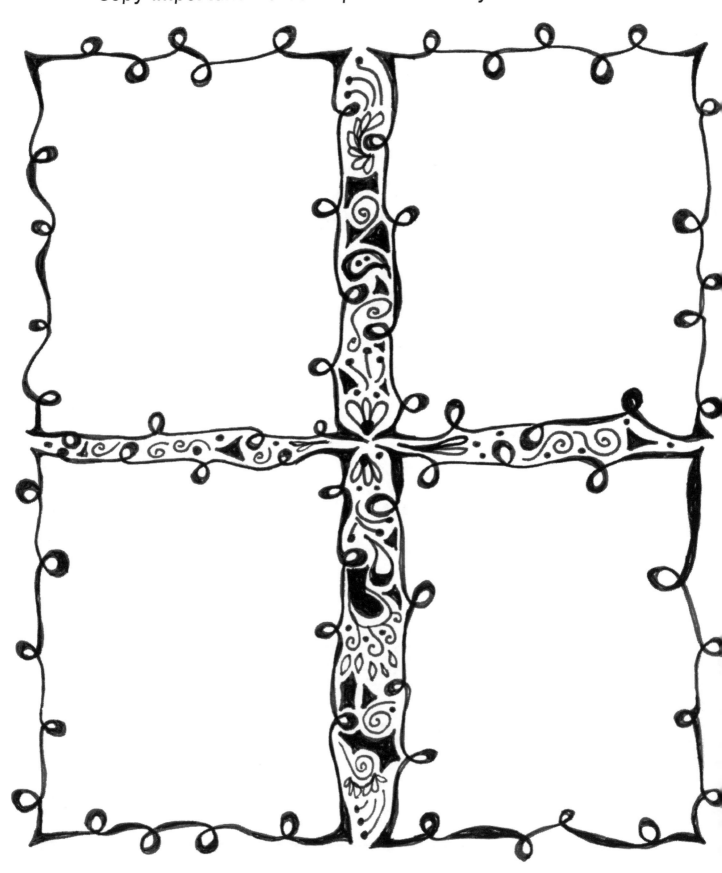

Spelling Time

Find 20 Words with **4** letters each.

Look in your books for words.

Write the words here:

DRAW A PICTURE
FROM ONE OF YOUR BOOKS:

COPYWORK

Find an interesting paragraph in one of your books and copy it. Be diligent to make your writing look exactly like it does in the book.

TITLE:_____

Page Number:_____

WRITE A STORY ABOUT THIS PICTURE

Circle Today's Date

January
February
March
April
May
June
July
August
September
October
November
December

1 2 3 4 5 6
7 8 9 10 11
12 13 14 15
16 17 18 19
20 21 22 23
24 25 26 27
28 29 30 31

MONDAY
TUESDAY
WEDNESDAY
THURSDAY
FRIDAY
SATURDAY
SUNDAY

2015
2016
2017
2018
2019
2020
2021
2022
2023
2024
2025
2026
2027
2028
2029

Write Today's Date: _____

Start Your Day!

Copy a Verse or Quote

_ _

_ _

_ _

_ _

_ _

To-Do List

LEARN TO DRAW HORSES

Look at the Drawing.

Draw the Missing Parts With a Smooth Black Pen.

Reading Time - 1 Hour (Set a timer)

Choose TWO Books - Read from each book for 30 minutes.

Copy important words or pictures from your book here:

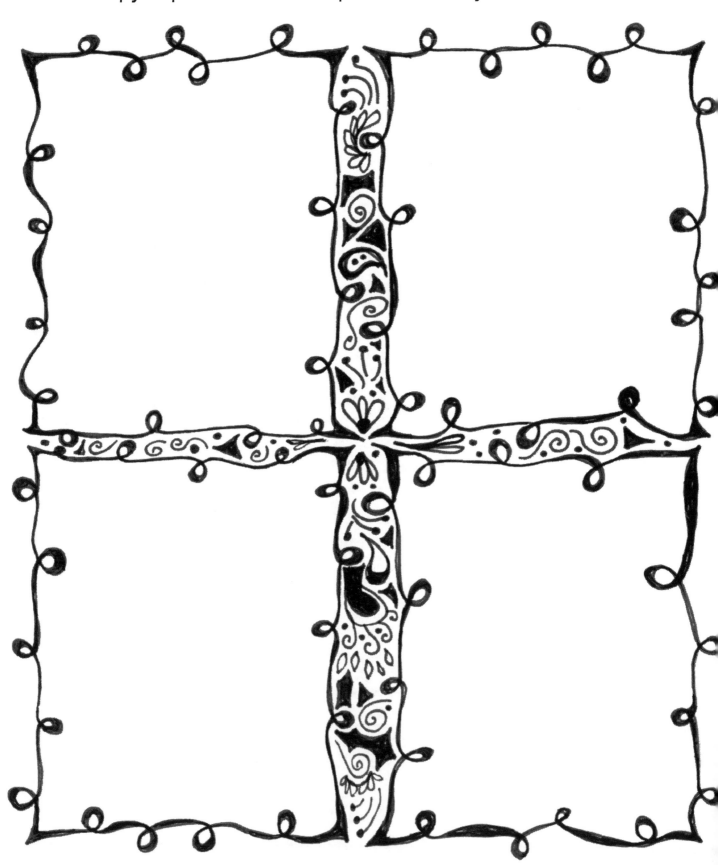

Spelling Time

Find 20 Words with 4 letters each.
Look in your books for words.
Write the words here:

Hopes, Dreams & Ideas

USE YOUR COLORED PENCILS

PRACTICE DRAWING HORSES

Circle Today's Date

January	1 2 3 4 5 6
February	7 8 9 10 11
March	12 13 14 15
April	16 17 18 19
May	20 21 22 23
June	24 25 26 27
July	28 29 30 31
August	
September	
October	
November	
December	

MONDAY
TUESDAY
WEDNESDAY
THURSDAY
FRIDAY
SATURDAY
SUNDAY

2015
2016
2017
2018
2019
2020
2021
2022
2023
2024
2025
2026
2027
2028
2029

Write Today's Date: _____

Start Your Day!

Copy a Verse or Quote

_____

_____

_____

_____

_____

To-Do List

_____

_____

_____

_____

_____

_____

_____

Favorite
Character:

_____

Watch a Documentary,
Or Movie about Horses.

TITLE:

Rate This
Film:

1 2 3 4 5

Tell the Whole Story with One Sentence:

Rating:
AWFUL
BAD
LAME
YUCKY
OKAY
NICE
GOOD
GREAT
SUPER
AMAZING

Draw Your Favorite Scene:

USE YOUR COLORED PENCILS

Nature Study

Go outside and make a realistic
drawing of something
you find in nature.

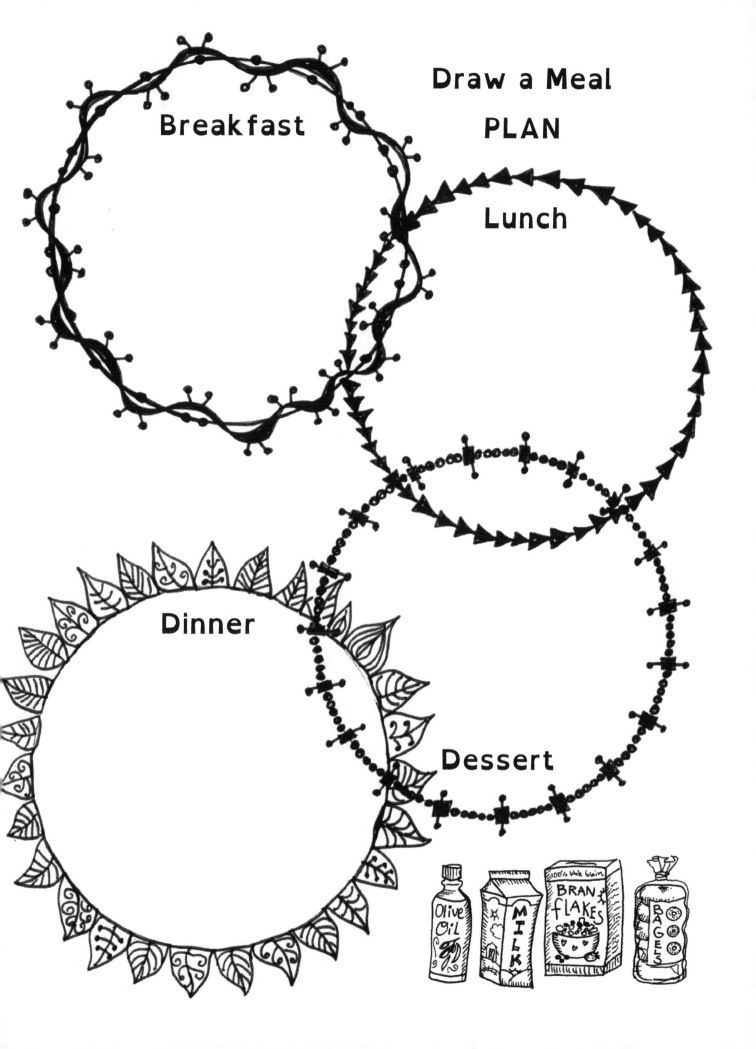

Breakfast

Draw a Meal
PLAN

Lunch

Dinner

Dessert

Reading Time - 1 Hour (Set a timer)
Choose TWO Books - Read from each book for 30 minutes.
Copy important words or pictures from your book here:

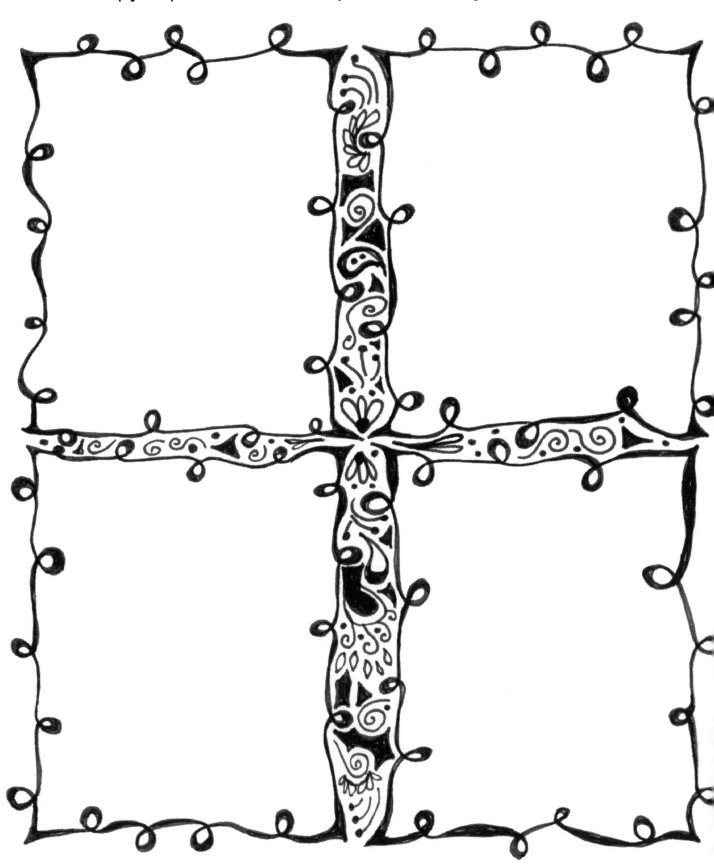

Spelling Time

Find 20 Words with 4 letters each.
Look in your books for words.
Write the words here:

_____   _____

_____   _____

_____   _____

_____   _____

_____   _____

_____   _____

_____   _____

_____   _____

_____   _____

_____   _____

DRAW A PICTURE
FROM ONE OF YOUR BOOKS:

COPYWORK

Find an interesting paragraph in one of your books and copy it. Be diligent to make your writing look exactly like it does in the book.

TITLE:_____

Page Number:_____

WRITE A STORY ABOUT THIS PICTURE

Circle Today's Date

January
February
March
April
May
June
July
August
September
October
November
December

1 2 3 4 5 6
7 8 9 10 11
12 13 14 15
16 17 18 19
20 21 22 23
24 25 26 27
28 29 30 31

MONDAY
TUESDAY
WEDNESDAY
THURSDAY
FRIDAY
SATURDAY
SUNDAY

2015
2016
2017
2018
2019
2020
2021
2022
2023
2024
2025
2026
2027
2028
2029

Write Today's Date: _____

Start Your Day!

Copy a Verse or Quote

_____
_____
_____
_____
_____

To-Do List

LEARN TO DRAW HORSES

Look at the Drawing.

Draw the Missing Parts With a Smooth Black Pen.

Reading Time - 1 Hour (Set a timer)

Choose TWO Books - Read from each book for 30 minutes.

Copy important words or pictures from your book here:

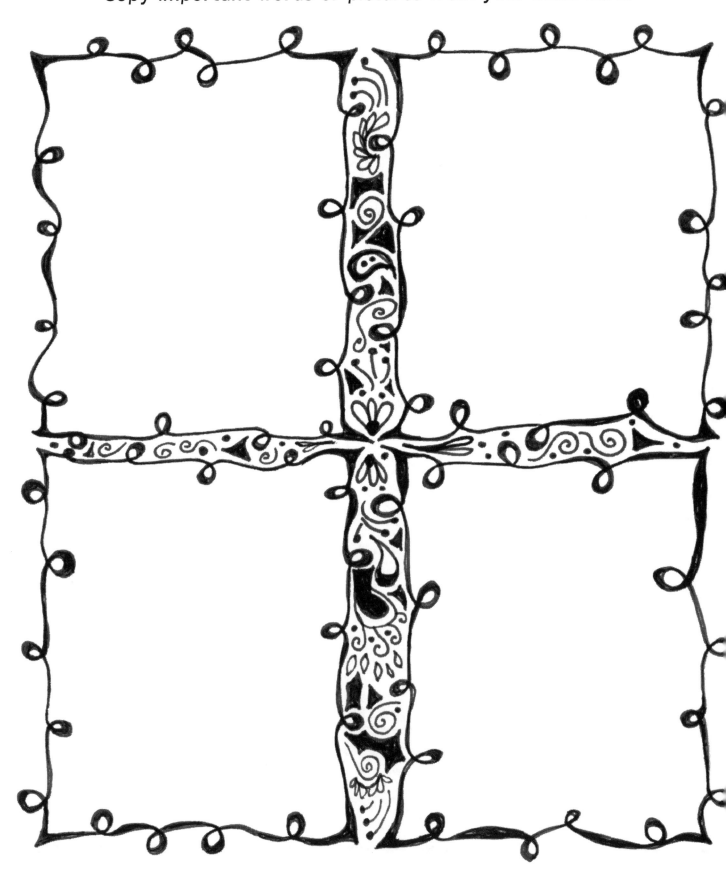

Spelling Time

Find 20 Words with 8 letters each.
Look in your books for words.
Write the words here:

_____   _____

_____   _____

_____   _____

_____   _____

_____   _____

_____   _____

_____   _____

_____   _____

_____   _____

Hopes, Dreams & Ideas

USE YOUR COLORED PENCILS

PRACTICE DRAWING HORSES

Circle Today's Date

January
February
March
April
May
June
July
August
September
October
November
December

1 2 3 4 5 6
7 8 9 10 11
12 13 14 15
16 17 18 19
20 21 22 23
24 25 26 27
28 29 30 31

MONDAY
TUESDAY
WEDNESDAY
THURSDAY
FRIDAY
SATURDAY
SUNDAY

2015
2016
2017
2018
2019
2020
2021
2022
2023
2024
2025
2026
2027
2028
2029

Write Today's Date: _ _ _ _ _ _ _ _ _ _ _ _ _ _ _

Start Your Day!

Copy a Verse or Quote

_____

_____

_____

_____

_____

To-Do List

Favorite Character:

_ _ _ _ _ _ _

Rate This Film:

1 2 3 4 5

Watch a Documentary, Or Movie about Horses.

TITLE:

Tell the Whole Story with One Sentence:

Draw Your Favorite Scene:

Rating:

AWFUL

BAD

LAME

YUCKY

OKAY

NICE

GOOD

GREAT

SUPER

AMAZING

Reading Time - 1 Hour (Set a timer)

Choose TWO Books - Read from each book for 30 minutes.

Copy important words or pictures from your book here:

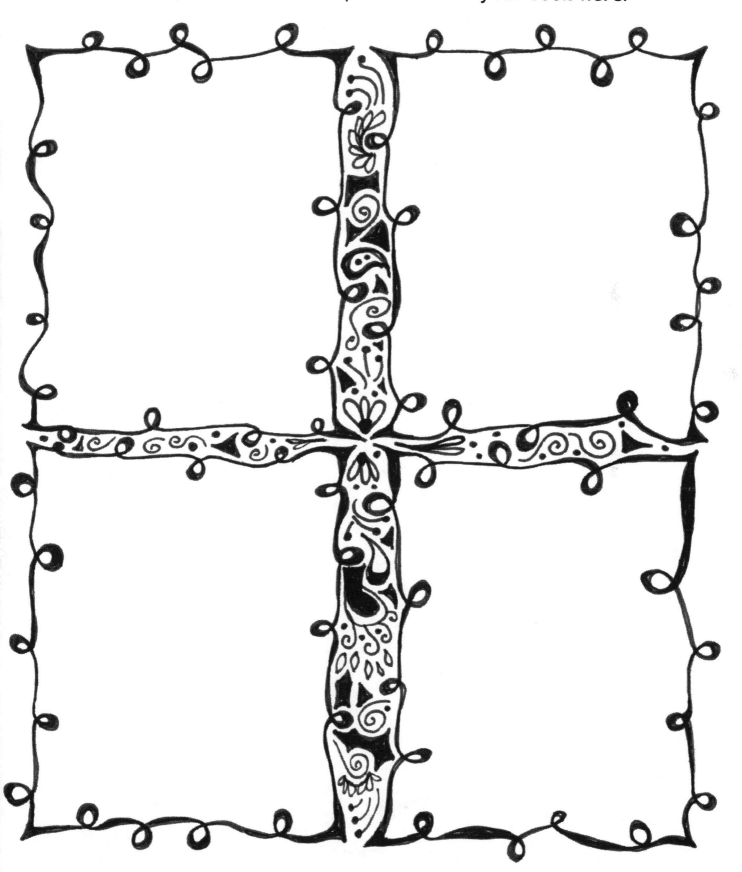

Nature Study

Go outside and make a realistic
drawing of something
you find in nature.

Fun With Letters! Just Add Color!

Listening Time

Listen to an audio book or classical music or
ask someone to read a story to you while
you color and draw on the next page.

What are you listening to?

_____

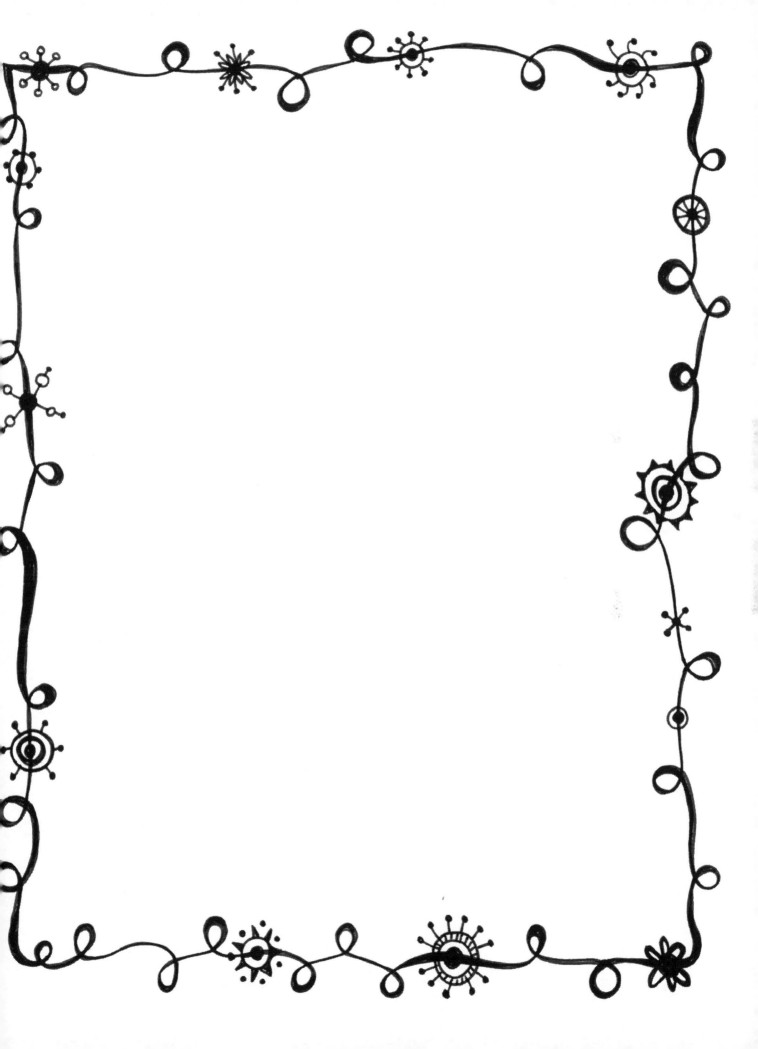

DRAW A PICTURE
FROM ONE OF YOUR BOOKS:

COPYWORK

Find an interesting paragraph in one of your books
and copy it. Be diligent to make your writing look
exactly like it does in the book.

TITLE:_____

Page Number:_____

WRITE A STORY ABOUT THIS PICTURE

INSTRUCTIONS

What do you want to learn about horses?

1.

2.

3.

4.

5.

Action Steps:

1. Go to the library or bookstore.

2. Bring home a stack of at least SIX interesting books about horses. Choose some that have diagrams, instructions and illustrations.

Supplies Needed:

You will need pencils, black drawing pens, colored pencils, gel pens and markers.

Choose SIX Books about Horses
To Use As School Books!

1. Write down the titles on each cover below.
2. Keep your stack of books in a safe place.
3. Be ready to read a few pages from your books daily.
4. Complete 10 pages each day in this workbook.

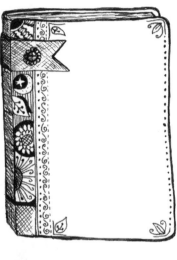 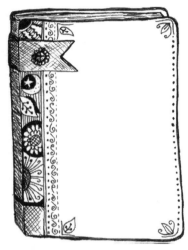 

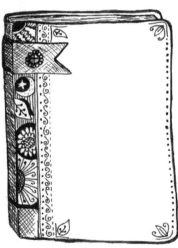  

Circle Today's Date

January
February
March
April
May
June
July
August
September
October
November
December

1 2 3 4 5 6
7 8 9 10 11
12 13 14 15
16 17 18 19
20 21 22 23
24 25 26 27
28 29 30 31

MONDAY
TUESDAY
WEDNESDAY
THURSDAY
FRIDAY
SATURDAY
SUNDAY

2015
2016
2017
2018
2019
2020
2021
2022
2023
2024
2025
2026
2027
2028
2029

Write Today's Date: _ _ _ _ _ _ _ _ _ _ _ _ _ _ _ _ _ _

Start Your Day!

Copy a Verse or Quote

_____

_____

_____

_____

_____

To-Do List

FUN PAGE

Fun With Letters! Just Add Color!

Reading Time - 1 Hour (Set a timer)

Choose TWO Books - Read from each book for 30 minutes.

Copy important words or pictures from your book here:

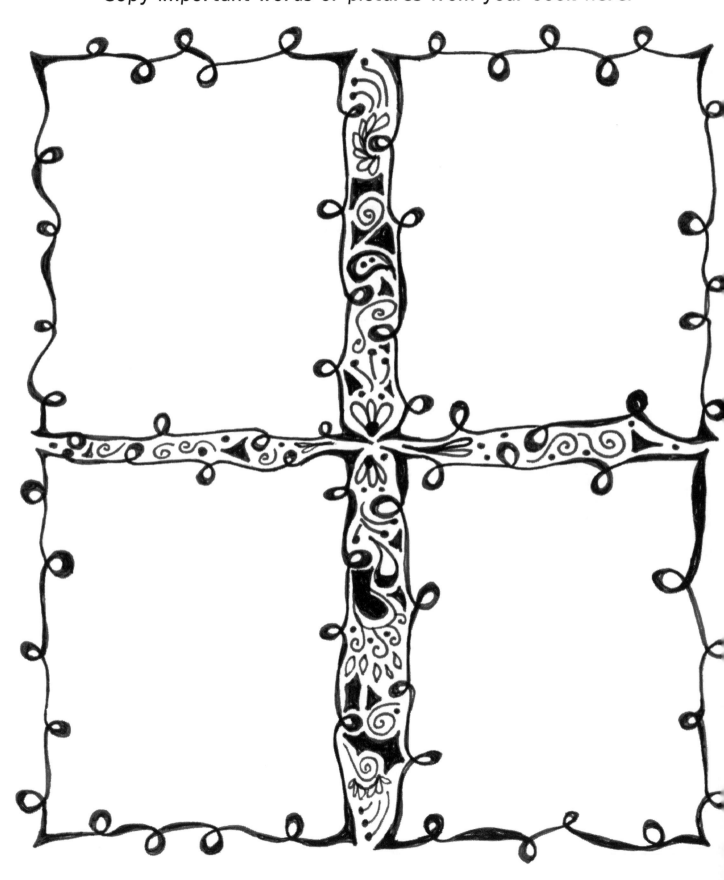

Spelling Time

Find 20 Words with 4 letters each.
Look in your books for words.
Write the words here:

Hopes, Dreams & Ideas

USE YOUR COLORED PENCILS

PRACTICE DRAWING HORSES

Circle Today's Date

January
February
March
April
May
June
July
August
September
October
November
December

1 2 3 4 5 6
7 8 9 10 11
12 13 14 15
16 17 18 19
20 21 22 23
24 25 26 27
28 29 30 31

MONDAY
TUESDAY
WEDNESDAY
THURSDAY
FRIDAY
SATURDAY
SUNDAY

2015
2016
2017
2018
2019
2020
2021
2022
2023
2024
2025
2026
2027
2028
2029

Write Today's Date: _ _ _ _ _ _ _ _ _ _ _ _ _ _ _ _

Start Your Day!

Copy a Verse or Quote

_____

_____

_____

_____

_____

To-Do List

_____

_____

_____

_____

_____

_____

_____

Favorite Character:

_____

Rate This Film:

1 2 3 4 5

Watch a Documentary, Or Movie about Horses.

TITLE:

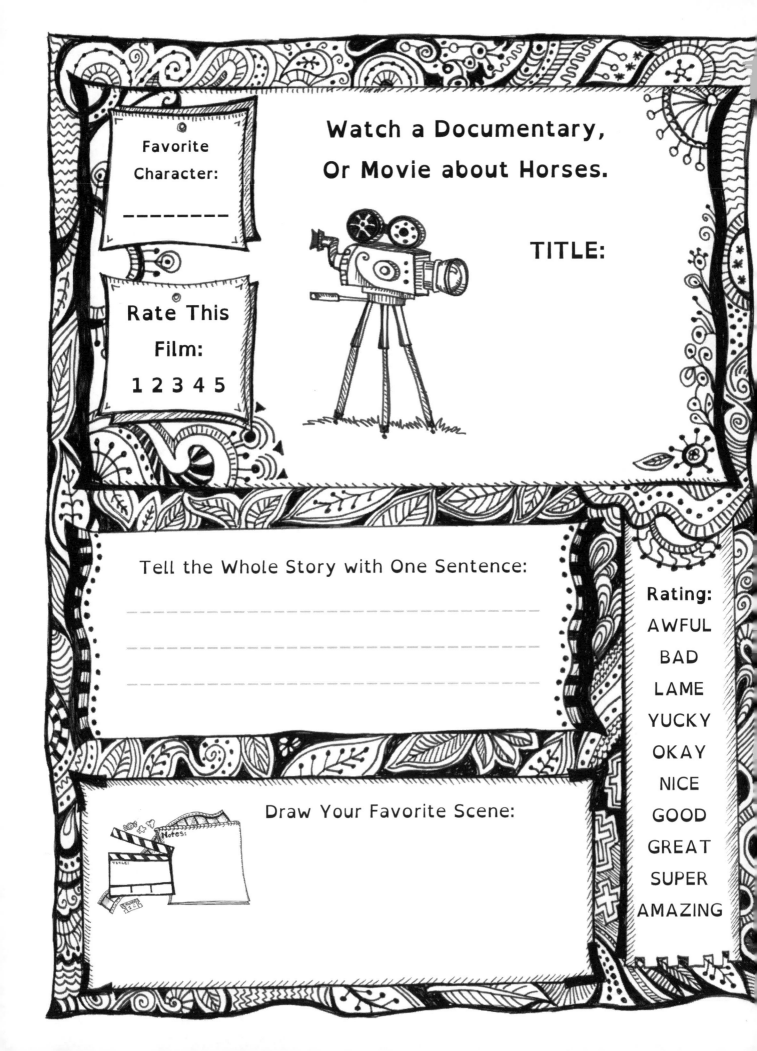

Tell the Whole Story with One Sentence:

Rating:

AWFUL

BAD

LAME

YUCKY

OKAY

NICE

GOOD

GREAT

SUPER

AMAZING

Draw Your Favorite Scene:

USE YOUR COLORED PENCILS

Nature Study

Go outside and make a realistic
drawing of something
you find in nature.

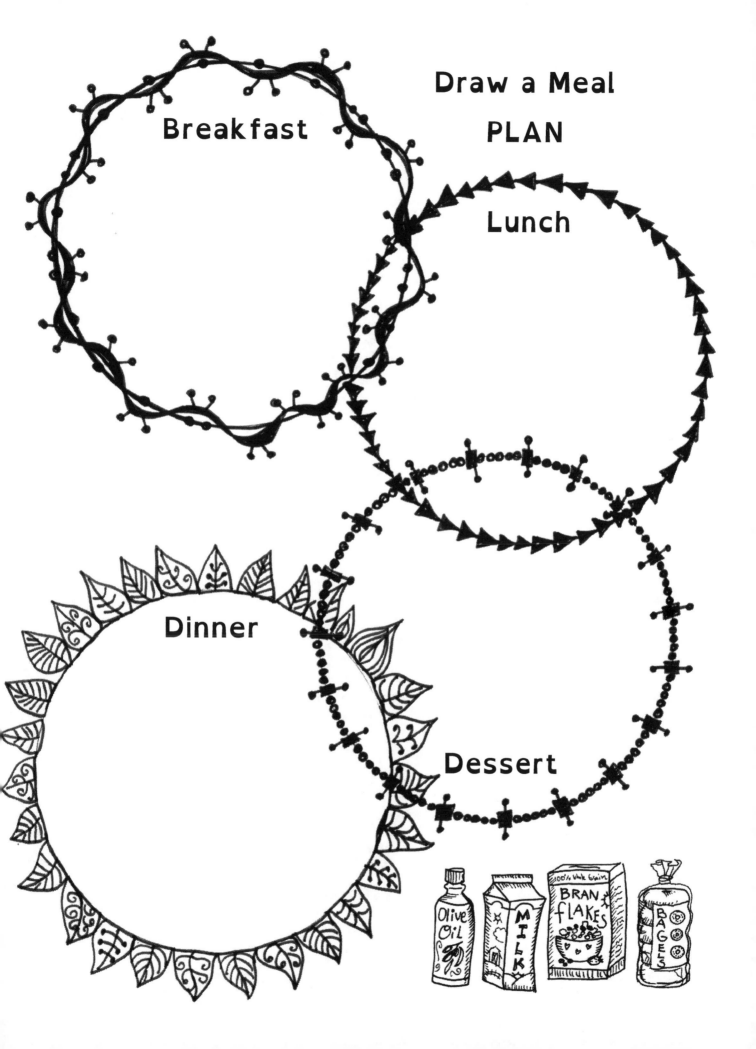

Breakfast

Draw a Meal
PLAN

Lunch

Dinner

Dessert

Reading Time - 1 Hour (Set a timer)

Choose TWO Books - Read from each book for 30 minutes.

Copy important words or pictures from your book here:

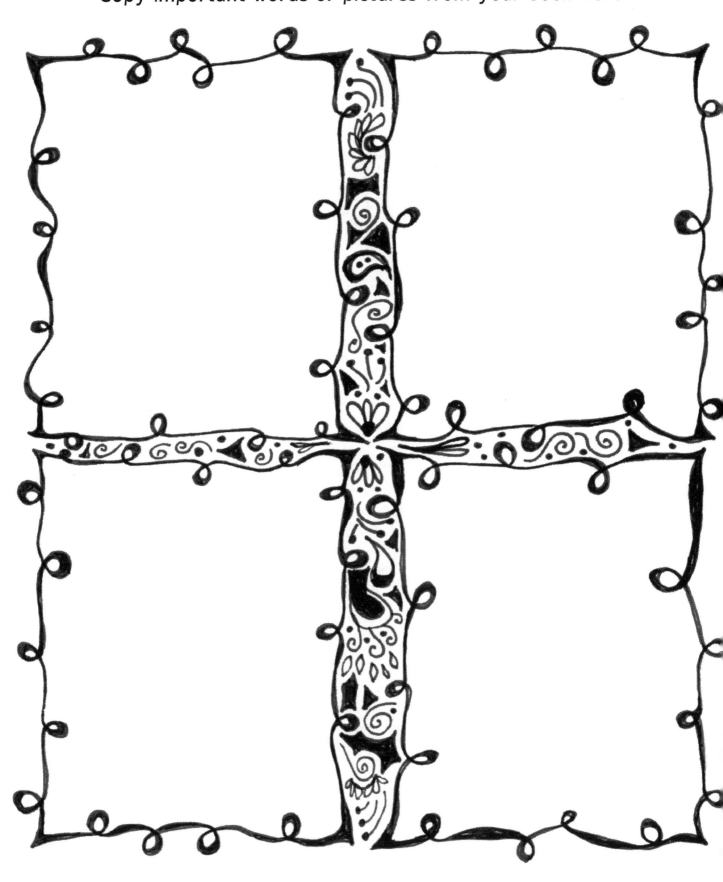

Fun With Letters! Just Add Color!

DRAW A PICTURE
FROM ONE OF YOUR BOOKS:

COPYWORK

Find an interesting paragraph in one of your books
and copy it. Be diligent to make your writing look
exactly like it does in the book.

TITLE:_____

Page Number:_____

WRITE A STORY ABOUT THIS PICTURE

Circle Today's Date

January
February
March
April
May
June
July
August
September
October
November
December

1 2 3 4 5 6
7 8 9 10 11
12 13 14 15
16 17 18 19
20 21 22 23
24 25 26 27
28 29 30 31

MONDAY
TUESDAY
WEDNESDAY
THURSDAY
FRIDAY
SATURDAY
SUNDAY

2015
2016
2017
2018
2019
2020
2021
2022
2023
2024
2025
2026
2027
2028
2029

Write Today's Date:_____

Start Your Day!

Copy a Verse or Quote

_____

_____

_____

_____

_____

To-Do List

_____

_____

_____

_____

_____

_____

Reading Time - 1 Hour (Set a timer)

Choose TWO Books - Read from each book for 30 minutes.

Copy important words or pictures from your book here:

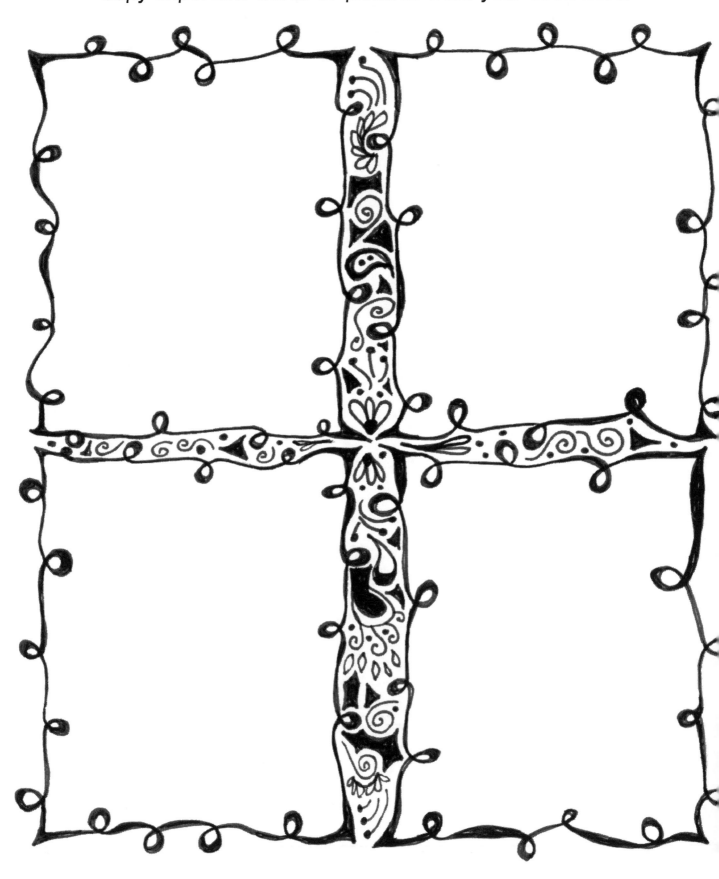

Spelling Time

Find 20 Words with **4** letters each.
Look in your books for words.
Write the words here:

_____   _____

_____   _____

_____   _____

_____   _____

_____   _____

_____   _____

_____   _____

_____   _____

_____   _____

_____   _____

Hopes, Dreams & Ideas

FUN PAGE

Listening Time

Listen to an audio book or classical music or
ask someone to read a story to you while
you color and draw on the next page.

What are you listening to?

_____

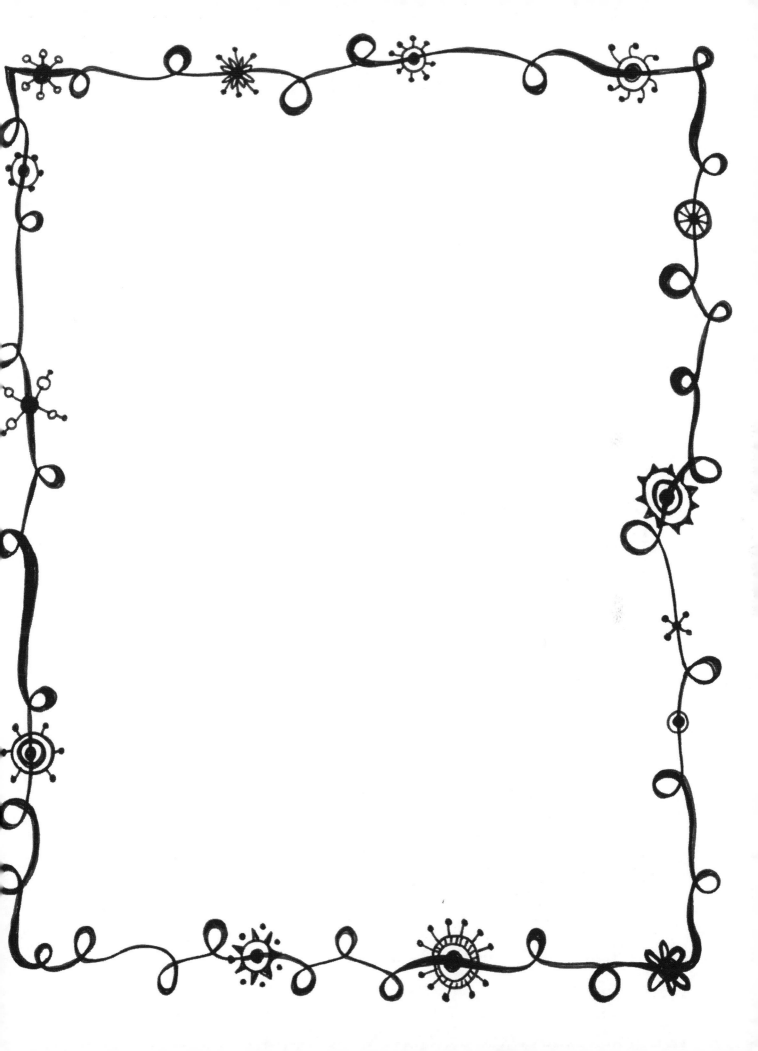

Circle Today's Date

January
February
March
April
May
June
July
August
September
October
November
December

1 2 3 4 5 6
7 8 9 10 11
12 13 14 15
16 17 18 19
20 21 22 23
24 25 26 27
28 29 30 31

MONDAY
TUESDAY
WEDNESDAY
THURSDAY
FRIDAY
SATURDAY
SUNDAY

2015
2016
2017
2018
2019
2020
2021
2022
2023
2024
2025
2026
2027
2028
2029

Write Today's Date: _ _ _ _ _ _ _ _ _ _ _ _ _ _ _ _

Start Your Day!

Copy a Verse or Quote

_____

_____

_____

_____

_____

To-Do List

_____

_____

_____

_____

_____

_____

Favorite Character:

_____

Watch a Documentary, Or Movie about Horses.

TITLE:

Rate This Film:

1 2 3 4 5

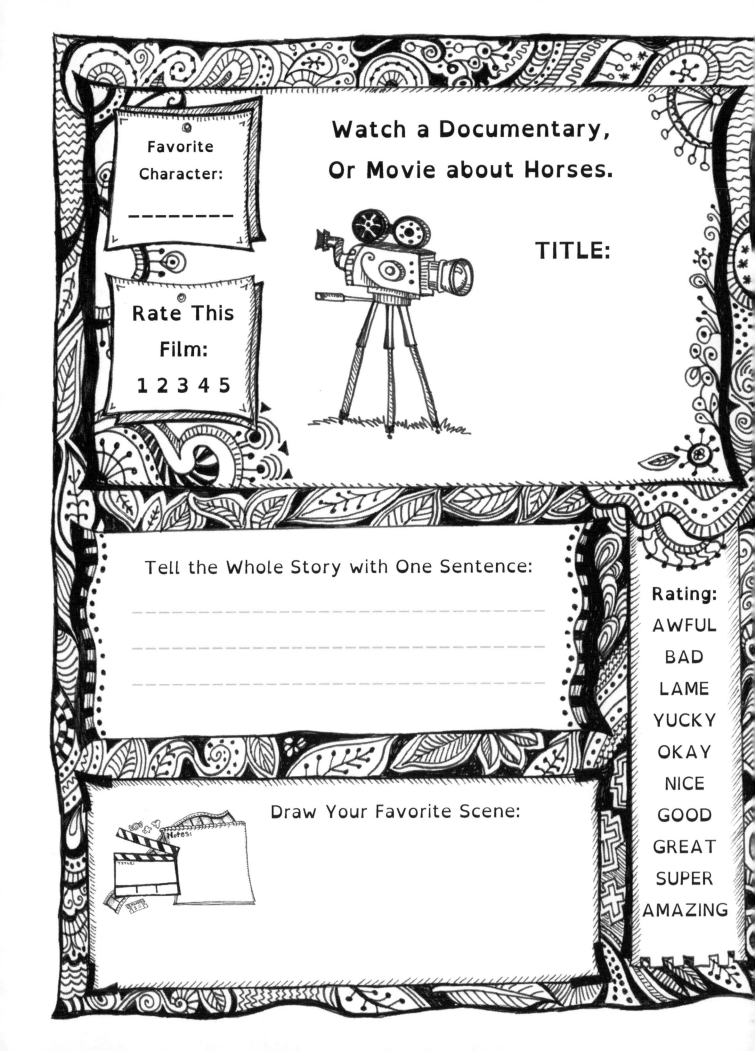

Tell the Whole Story with One Sentence:

Rating:

AWFUL

BAD

LAME

YUCKY

OKAY

NICE

GOOD

GREAT

SUPER

AMAZING

Draw Your Favorite Scene:

Notes:

Nature Study

Go outside and make a realistic
drawing of something
you find in nature.

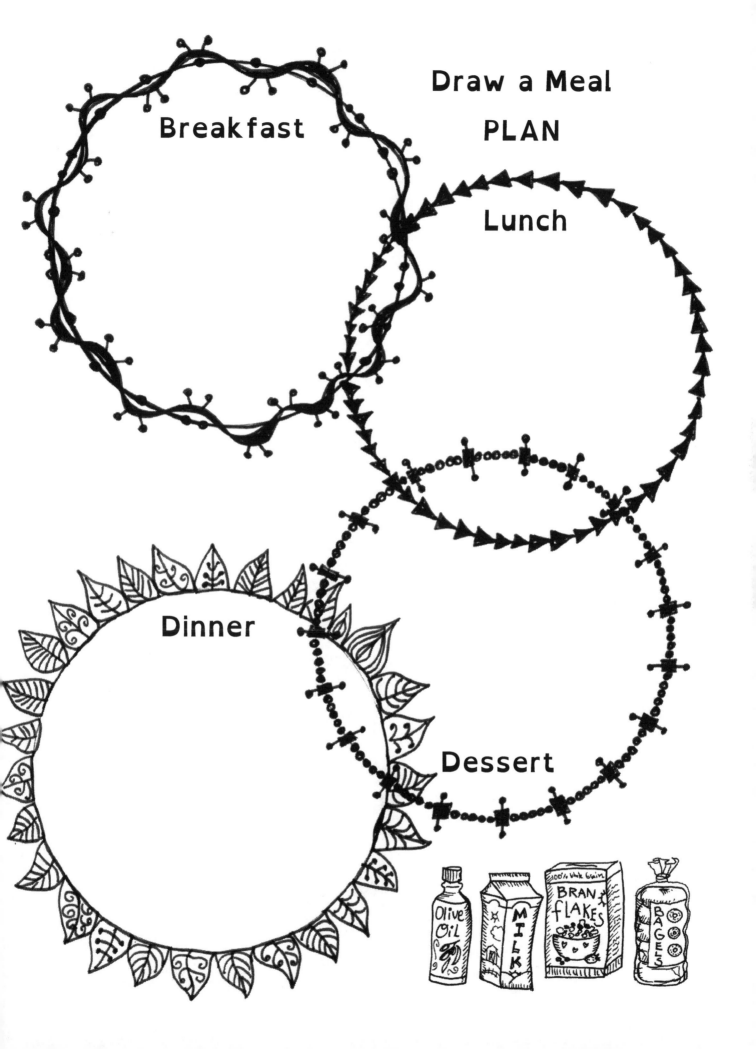

Reading Time - 1 Hour (Set a timer)

Choose TWO Books - Read from each book for 30 minutes.

Copy important words or pictures from your book here:

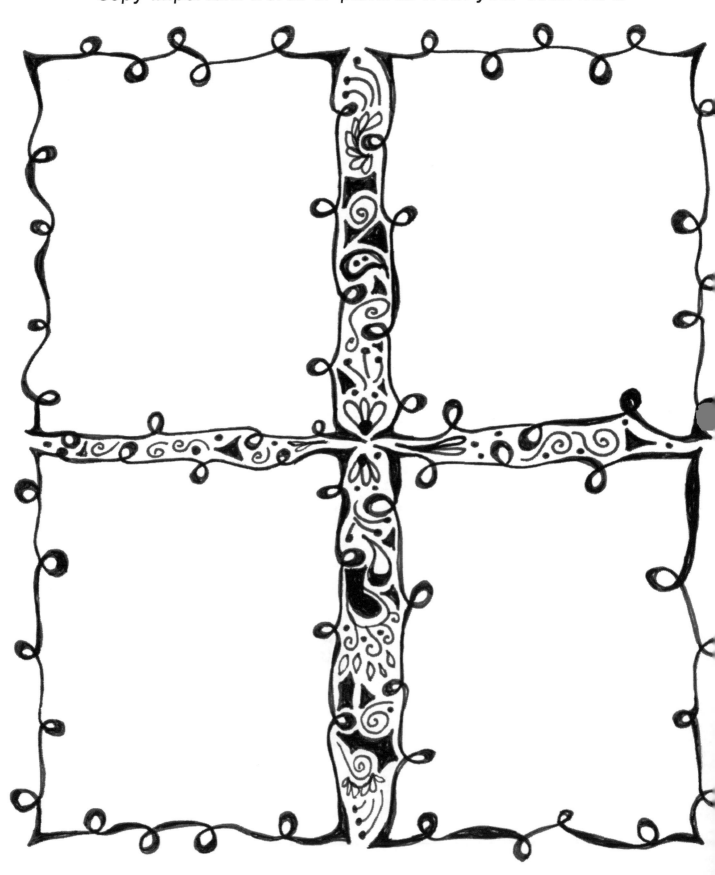

Spelling Time

Find 20 Words with **6** letters each.

Look in your books for words.

Write the words here:

DRAW A PICTURE
FROM ONE OF YOUR BOOKS:

COPYWORK

Find an interesting paragraph in one of your books and copy it. Be diligent to make your writing look exactly like it does in the book.

TITLE:_____

Page Number:_____

WRITE A STORY ABOUT THIS PICTURE

Circle Today's Date

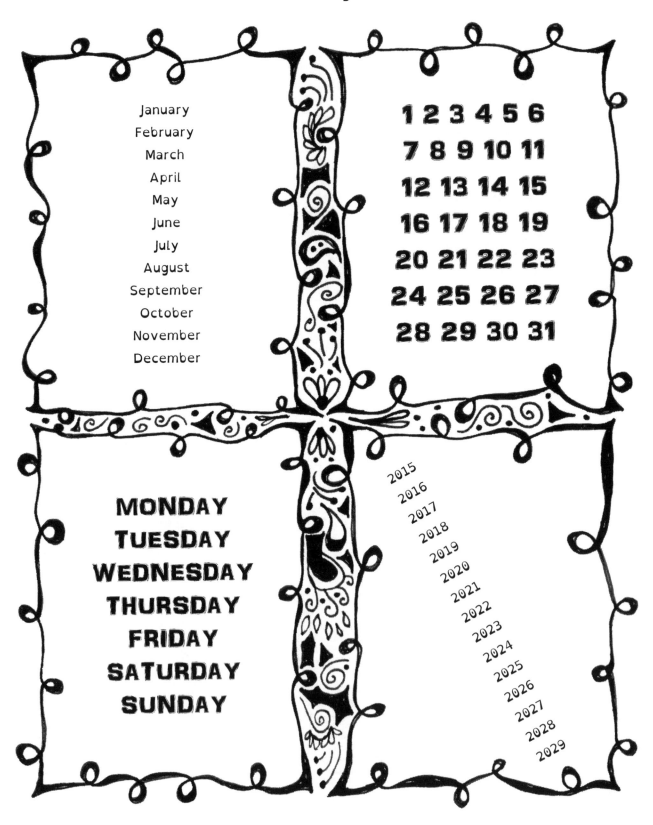

January
February
March
April
May
June
July
August
September
October
November
December

1 2 3 4 5 6
7 8 9 10 11
12 13 14 15
16 17 18 19
20 21 22 23
24 25 26 27
28 29 30 31

MONDAY
TUESDAY
WEDNESDAY
THURSDAY
FRIDAY
SATURDAY
SUNDAY

2015
2016
2017
2018
2019
2020
2021
2022
2023
2024
2025
2026
2027
2028
2029

Write Today's Date: _ _ _ _ _ _ _ _ _ _ _ _ _ _ _

Start Your Day!

Copy a Verse or Quote

_ _ _ _ _ _ _ _ _ _ _ _ _ _ _ _ _ _ _ _

_ _ _ _ _ _ _ _ _ _ _ _ _ _ _ _ _ _ _ _

_ _ _ _ _ _ _ _ _ _ _ _ _ _ _ _ _ _ _ _

_ _ _ _ _ _ _ _ _ _ _ _ _ _ _ _ _ _ _ _

_ _ _ _ _ _ _ _ _ _ _ _ _ _ _ _ _ _ _ _

To-Do List

LEARN TO DRAW HORSES

Look at the Drawing.

Trace the Drawing

Draw the Missing Parts With a Smooth Black Pen.

Draw it Yourself.

Reading Time - 1 Hour (Set a timer)

Choose TWO Books - Read from each book for 30 minutes.

Copy important words or pictures from your book here:

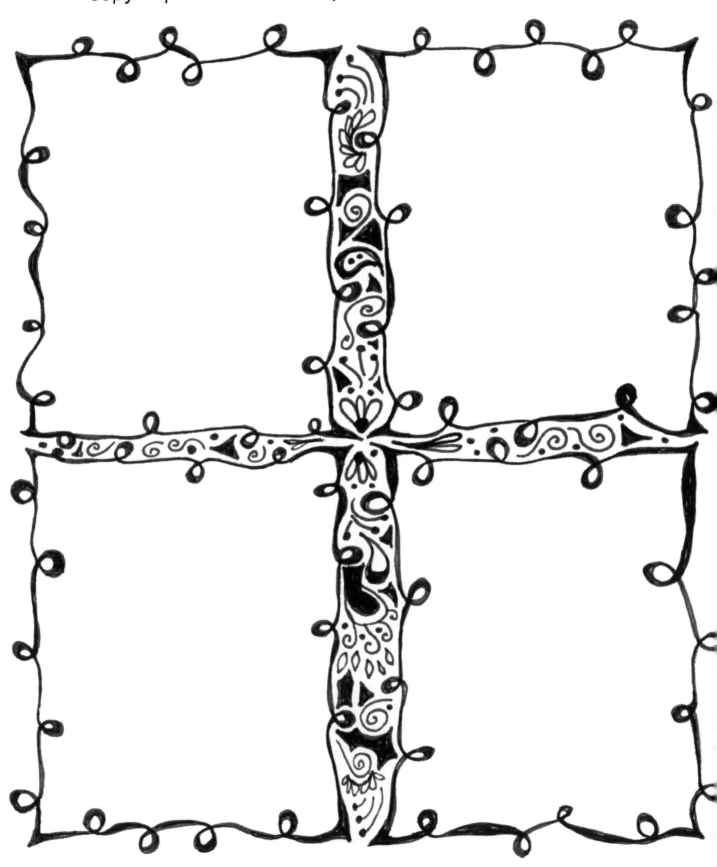

Spelling Time

Find 20 Words with **5** letters each.

Look in your books for words.

Write the words here:

Hopes, Dreams & Ideas

PRACTICE DRAWING HORSES

Circle Today's Date

January
February
March
April
May
June
July
August
September
October
November
December

1 2 3 4 5 6
7 8 9 10 11
12 13 14 15
16 17 18 19
20 21 22 23
24 25 26 27
28 29 30 31

MONDAY
TUESDAY
WEDNESDAY
THURSDAY
FRIDAY
SATURDAY
SUNDAY

2015
2016
2017
2018
2019
2020
2021
2022
2023
2024
2025
2026
2027
2028
2029

Write Today's Date: _____

Start Your Day!

Copy a Verse or Quote

_____

_____

_____

_____

_____

To-Do List

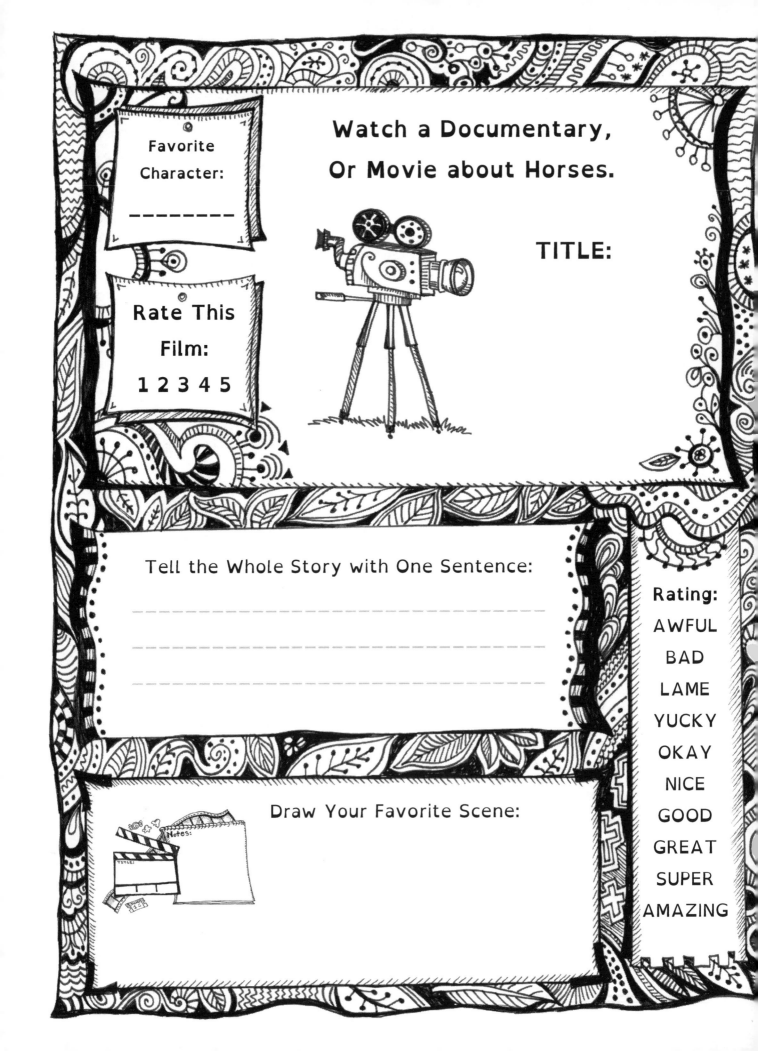

Favorite Character:

_____

Rate This Film:

1 2 3 4 5

Watch a Documentary, Or Movie about Horses.

TITLE:

Tell the Whole Story with One Sentence:

Draw Your Favorite Scene:

Notes:

Rating:

AWFUL

BAD

LAME

YUCKY

OKAY

NICE

GOOD

GREAT

SUPER

AMAZING

USE YOUR COLORED PENCILS

Nature Study

Go outside and make a realistic
drawing of something
you find in nature.

Fun With Letters! Just Add Color!

Reading Time - 1 Hour (Set a timer)

Choose TWO Books - Read from each book for 30 minutes.

Copy important words or pictures from your book here:

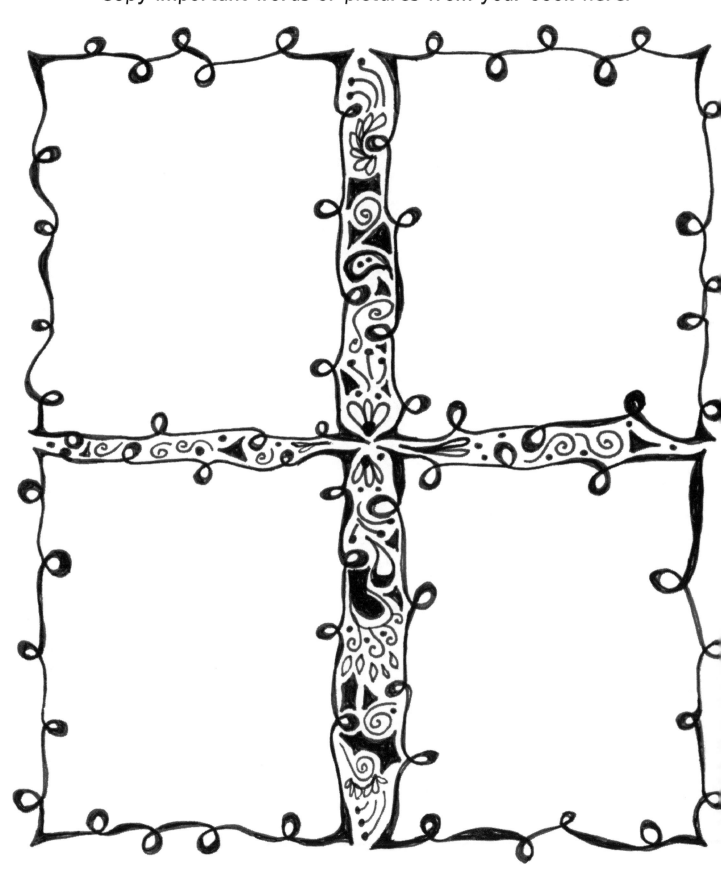

Spelling Time

Find 20 Words with **4** letters each.

Look in your books for words.

Write the words here:

_____   _____

_____   _____

_____   _____

_____   _____

_____   _____

_____   _____

_____   _____

_____   _____

_____   _____

DRAW A PICTURE
FROM ONE OF YOUR BOOKS:

COPYWORK

Find an interesting paragraph in one of your books and copy it. Be diligent to make your writing look exactly like it does in the book.

TITLE:_____

Page Number:_____

WRITE A STORY ABOUT THIS PICTURE

Circle Today's Date

January
February
March
April
May
June
July
August
September
October
November
December

1 2 3 4 5 6
7 8 9 10 11
12 13 14 15
16 17 18 19
20 21 22 23
24 25 26 27
28 29 30 31

MONDAY
TUESDAY
WEDNESDAY
THURSDAY
FRIDAY
SATURDAY
SUNDAY

2015
2016
2017
2018
2019
2020
2021
2022
2023
2024
2025
2026
2027
2028
2029

Write Today's Date: _____

Start Your Day!

Copy a Verse or Quote

_____

_____

_____

_____

_____

To-Do List

_____

_____

_____

_____

_____

_____

_____

LEARN TO DRAW HORSES

Look at the Drawing.

Draw the Missing Parts With a Smooth Black Pen.

Reading Time - 1 Hour (Set a timer)

Choose TWO Books - Read from each book for 30 minutes.

Copy important words or pictures from your book here:

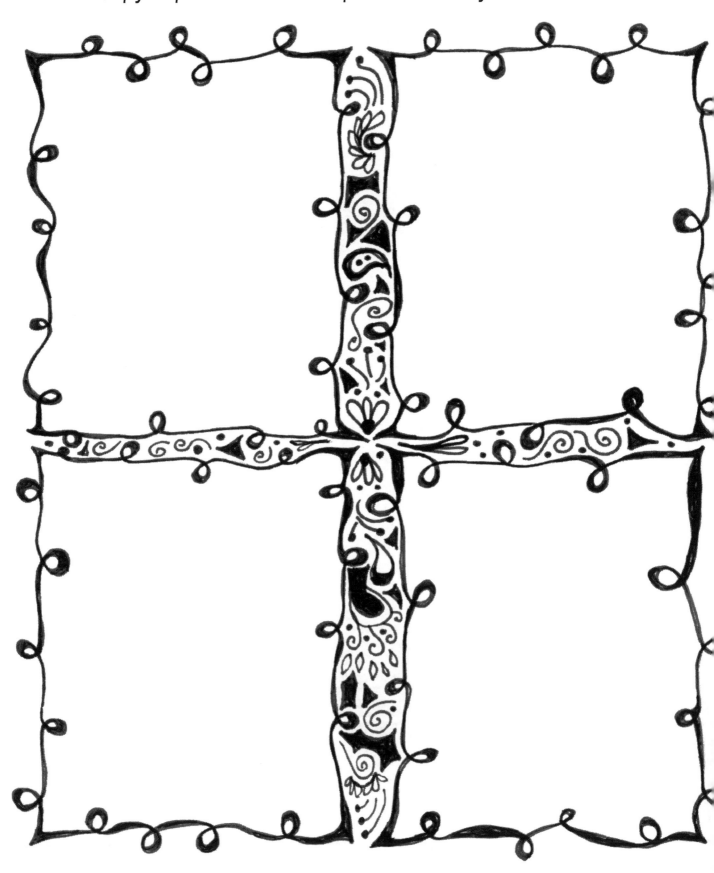

Spelling Time

Find 20 Words with **4** letters each.
Look in your books for words.
Write the words here:

Hopes, Dreams & Ideas

PRACTICE DRAWING HORSES

Circle Today's Date

January
February
March
April
May
June
July
August
September
October
November
December

1 2 3 4 5 6
7 8 9 10 11
12 13 14 15
16 17 18 19
20 21 22 23
24 25 26 27
28 29 30 31

MONDAY
TUESDAY
WEDNESDAY
THURSDAY
FRIDAY
SATURDAY
SUNDAY

2015
2016
2017
2018
2019
2020
2021
2022
2023
2024
2025
2026
2027
2028
2029

Write Today's Date: _ _ _ _ _ _ _ _ _ _ _ _ _ _ _

Start Your Day!

Copy a Verse or Quote

To-Do List

Favorite
Character:

_____

Rate This
Film:

1 2 3 4 5

Watch a Documentary,
Or Movie about Horses.

TITLE:

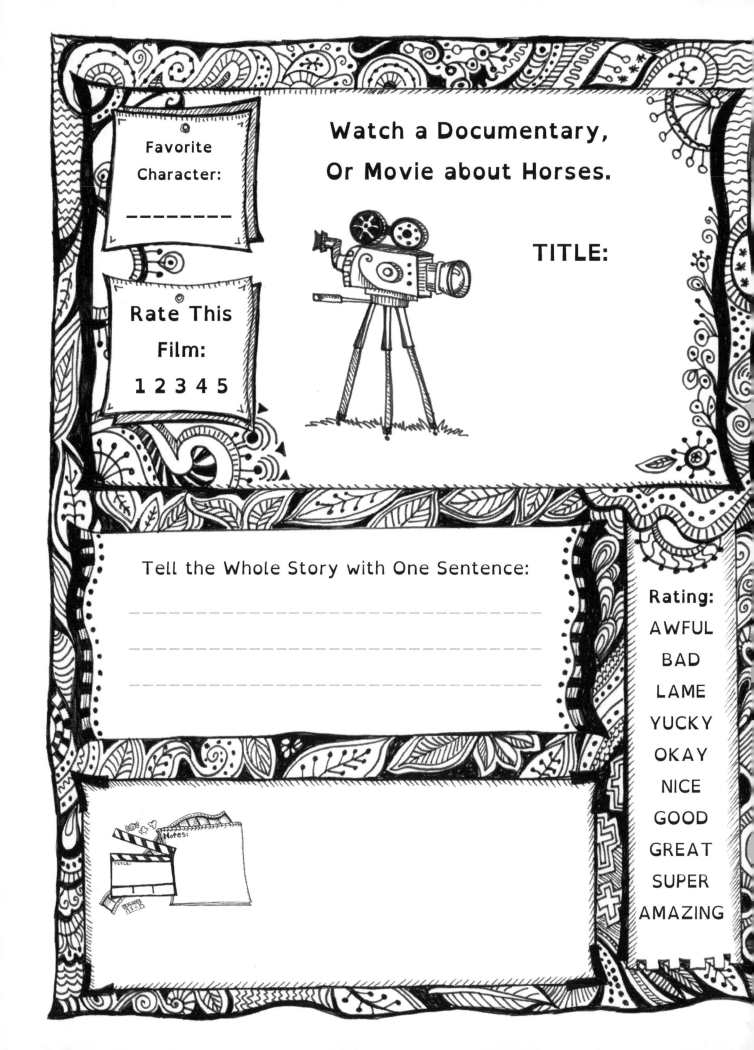

Tell the Whole Story with One Sentence:

_____

_____

_____

Notes:

Rating:

AWFUL

BAD

LAME

YUCKY

OKAY

NICE

GOOD

GREAT

SUPER

AMAZING

Draw Your Favorite Scene:

Nature Study

Go outside and make a realistic
drawing of something
you find in nature.

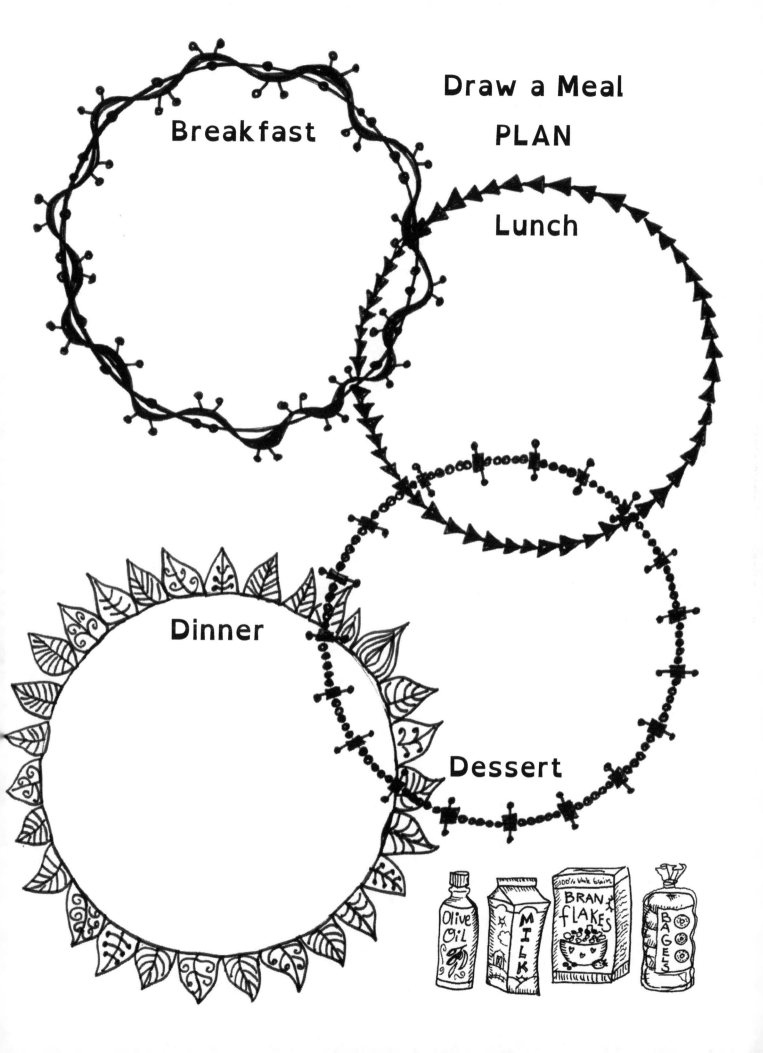

Reading Time - 1 Hour (Set a timer)

Choose TWO Books - Read from each book for 30 minutes.
Copy important words or pictures from your book here:

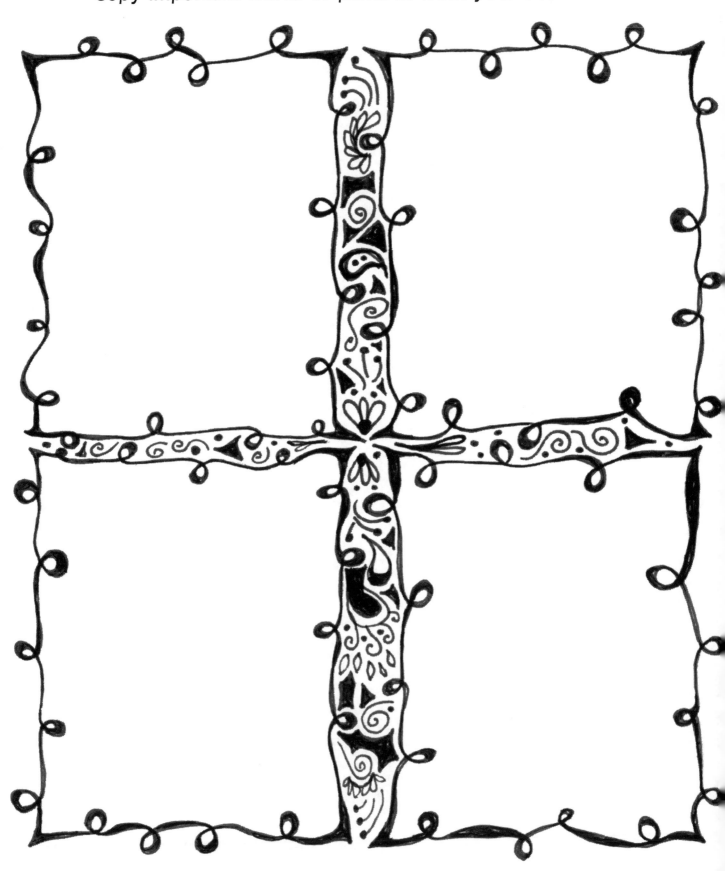

Spelling Time

Find 20 Words with 7 letters each.
Look in your books for words.
Write the words here:

_____   _____

_____   _____

_____   _____

_____   _____

_____   _____

_____   _____

_____   _____

_____   _____

_____   _____

DRAW A PICTURE
FROM ONE OF YOUR BOOKS:

COPYWORK

Find an interesting paragraph in one of your books and copy it. Be diligent to make your writing look exactly like it does in the book.

TITLE:_____

Page Number:_____

WRITE A STORY ABOUT THIS PICTURE

Circle Today's Date

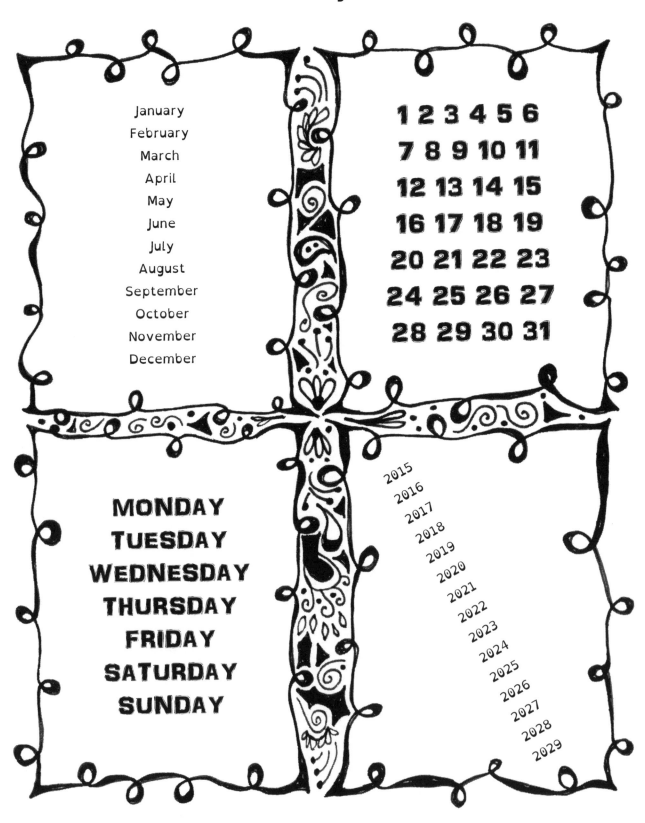

January
February
March
April
May
June
July
August
September
October
November
December

1 2 3 4 5 6
7 8 9 10 11
12 13 14 15
16 17 18 19
20 21 22 23
24 25 26 27
28 29 30 31

MONDAY
TUESDAY
WEDNESDAY
THURSDAY
FRIDAY
SATURDAY
SUNDAY

2015
2016
2017
2018
2019
2020
2021
2022
2023
2024
2025
2026
2027
2028
2029

Write Today's Date: _ _ _ _ _ _ _ _ _ _ _ _ _ _ _ _ _ _

Start Your Day!

Copy a Verse or Quote

- -

- -

- -

- -

- -

To-Do List

LEARN TO DRAW HORSES

Look at the Drawing.

Draw the Missing Parts With a Smooth Black Pen.

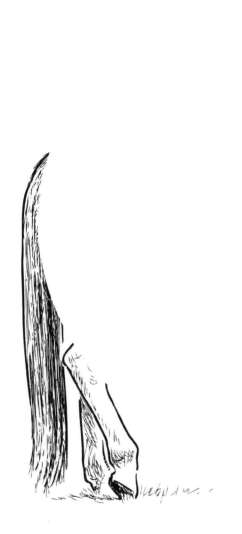

Reading Time - 1 Hour (Set a timer)

Choose TWO Books - Read from each book for 30 minutes.

Copy important words or pictures from your book here:

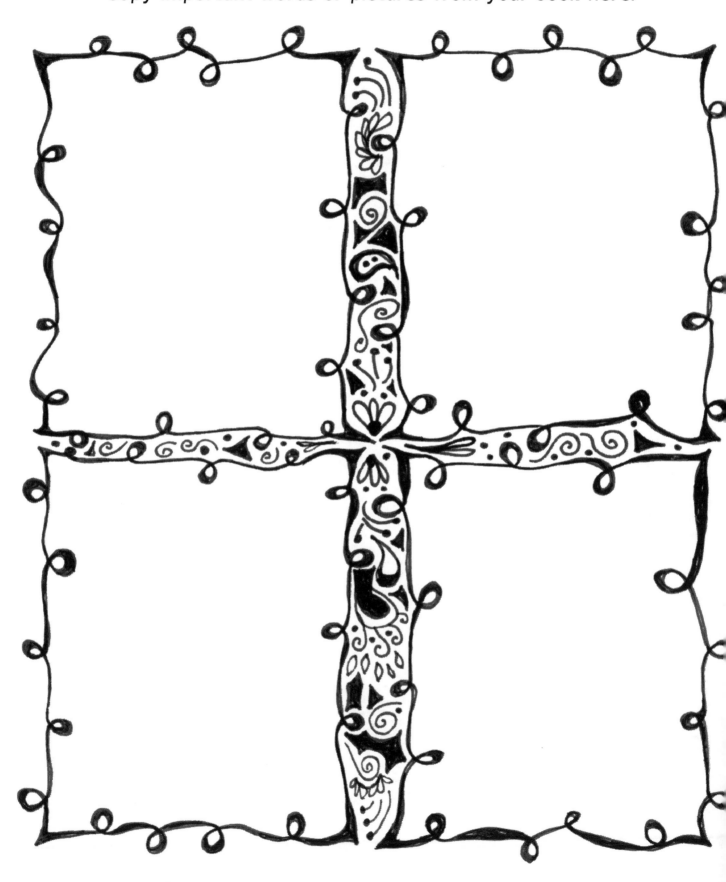

Spelling Time

Find 20 Words with 4 letters each.

Look in your books for words.

Write the words here:

_____   _____

_____   _____

_____   _____

_____   _____

_____   _____

_____   _____

_____   _____

_____   _____

_____   _____

_____   _____

Hopes, Dreams & Ideas

PRACTICE DRAWING HORSES

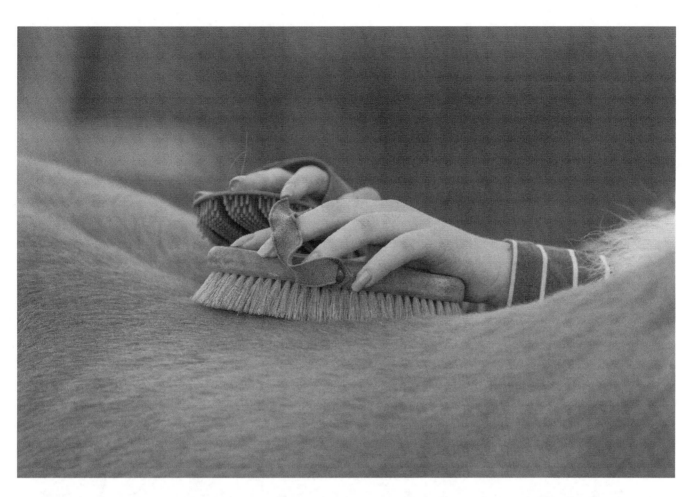

Circle Today's Date

January
February
March
April
May
June
July
August
September
October
November
December

1 2 3 4 5 6
7 8 9 10 11
12 13 14 15
16 17 18 19
20 21 22 23
24 25 26 27
28 29 30 31

MONDAY
TUESDAY
WEDNESDAY
THURSDAY
FRIDAY
SATURDAY
SUNDAY

2015
2016
2017
2018
2019
2020
2021
2022
2023
2024
2025
2026
2027
2028
2029

Write Today's Date: _ _ _ _ _ _ _ _ _ _ _ _ _ _

Start Your Day!

Copy a Verse or Quote

_____

_____

_____

_____

_____

To-Do List

Favorite Character:

_____

Rate This Film:

1 2 3 4 5

Watch a Documentary, Or Movie about Horses.

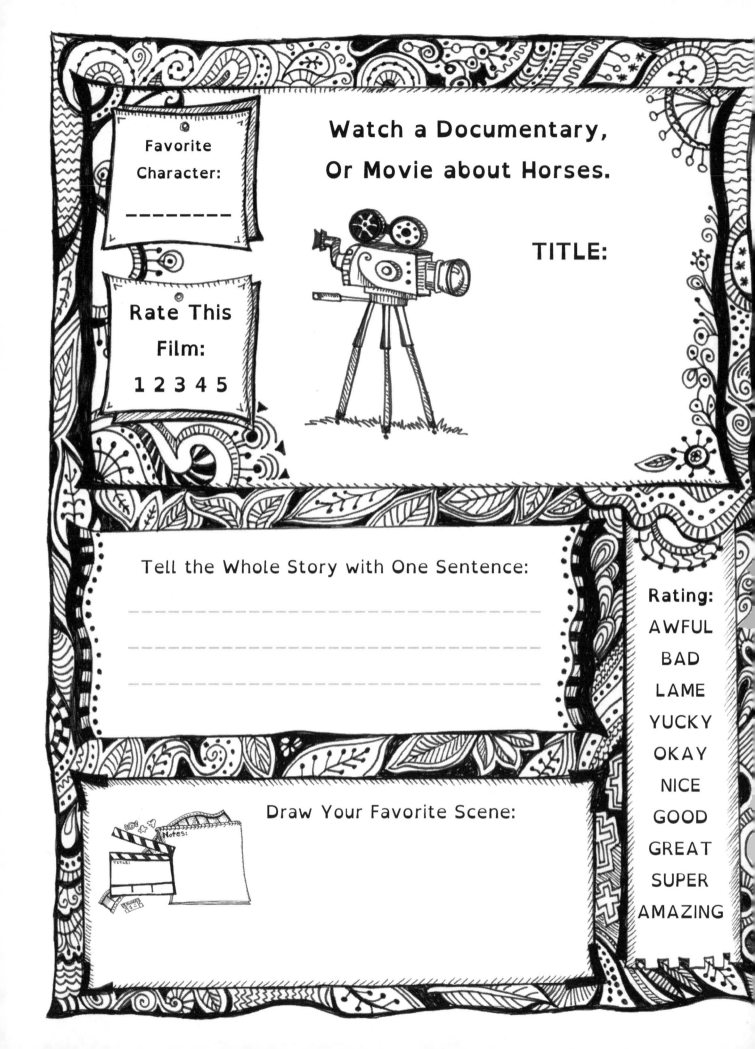

TITLE:

Tell the Whole Story with One Sentence:

Rating:

AWFUL

BAD

LAME

YUCKY

OKAY

NICE

GOOD

GREAT

SUPER

AMAZING

Draw Your Favorite Scene:

Nature Study

Go outside and make a realistic
drawing of something
you find in nature.

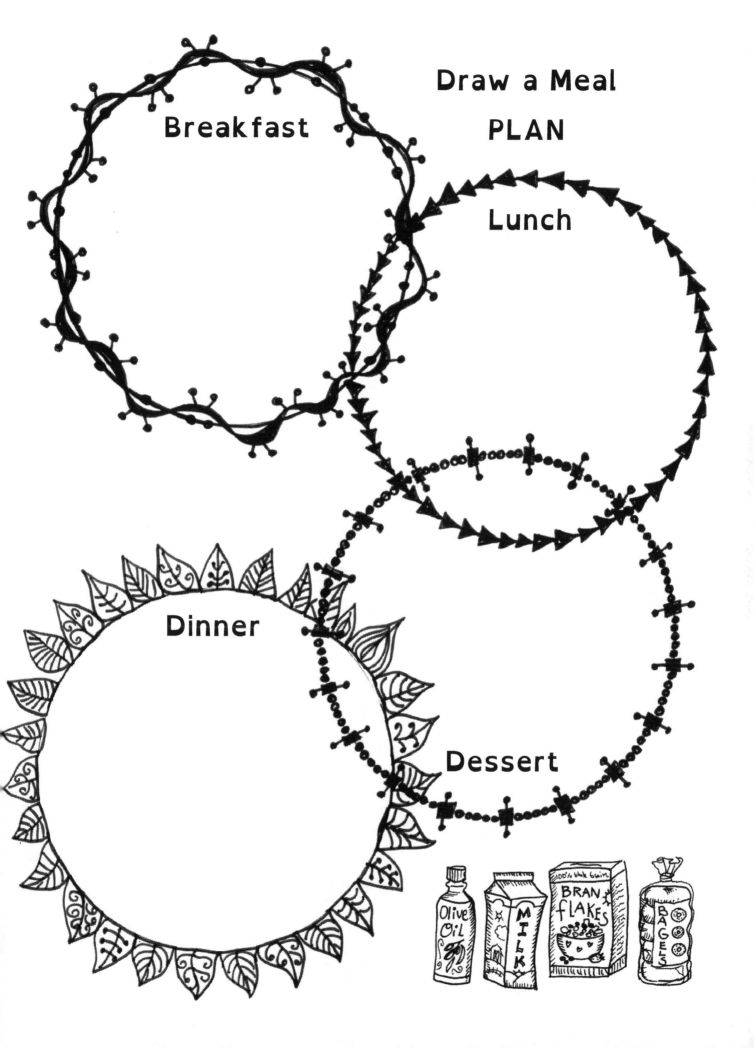

Reading Time - 1 Hour (Set a timer)

Choose TWO Books - Read from each book for 30 minutes.

Copy important words or pictures from your book here:

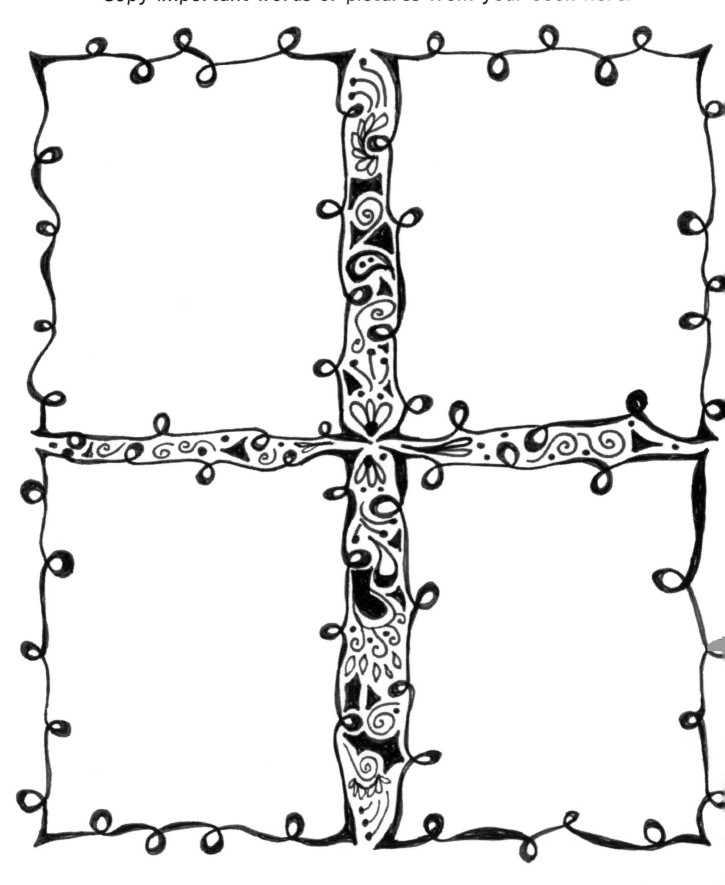

Spelling Time

Find 20 Words with **4** letters each.

Look in your books for words.

Write the words here:

DRAW A PICTURE
FROM ONE OF YOUR BOOKS:

COPYWORK

Find an interesting paragraph in one of your books and copy it. Be diligent to make your writing look exactly like it does in the book.

TITLE:_____

Page Number:_____

Do It Yourself
HOMESCHOOL
JOURNALS

Copyright Information

Do It YOURSELF Homeschool Journal, and electronic printable downloads are for Home and Family use only. You may make copies of these materials for only the children in your household.

All other uses of this material must be permitted in writing by the Thinking Tree LLC. It is a violation of copyright law to distribute the electronic files or make copies for your friends, associates or students without our permission.

For information on using these materials for businesses, co-ops, summer camps, day camps, daycare, afterschool program, churches, or schools please contact us for licensing.

Contact Us:

The Thinking Tree LLC

617 N. Swope St. Greenfield, IN 46140. United States

317.622.8852 PHONE (Dial +1 outside of the USA) 267.712.7889 FAX

www.DyslexiaGames.com

jbrown@DyslexiaGames.com

Made in the USA
Charleston, SC
25 February 2016